STEP-BY-STEP

Furniture Finishing

By Nancy Howell-Koehler

Golden Press • New York
Western Publishing Company, Inc.
Racine, Wisconsin

This stitched, stuffed, and painted creation, "The Love Affair or the Cow Pasture Bed," by Michelle Gamm Clifton, explores the possibilities of furniture as art.

Art Director: Remo Cosentino
Art Assistant: Diane Wagner
Diagrams: Gary Tong
Editor: Caroline Greenberg
Photographs: John Garetti

Library of Congress Catalog Card Number: 74–82072

Contents

Introduction

When man won his evolutionary battle to stand erect, he acquired the need to rest in a sitting position. Nature gave him his first seats in the form of logs, rocks, and the like. In time he learned to make his own chairs and other furniture.

Down through the generations, people have inherited the furniture of their ancestors—sometimes respecting it, sometimes disdaining it, sometimes discarding it. But never in history has the need to preserve and restore the irreplaceable wooden furniture of the past been more apparent than today.

Wood, more specifically hardwood, is no longer plentiful. Skilled labor is no longer cheap. Finely crafted solid-wood furniture is a great luxury today. Out of necessity, we are challenged to make innovative use of our old furniture as well as our mass-produced unfinished furniture. Nor is economics the only consideration. Our swiftly changing way of life and increasingly rootless existence have underlined the importance of preserving such links with the past as our heritage of hardwood furniture.

An interest in restoring furniture often comes about because of a specific need. An inherited rocker in poor repair, a spot-ringed coffee table, a crudely painted pine chest may bring you face-to-face with the need to know the techniques of refinishing and restoration. Or perhaps the expense of buying new furniture makes the art of recycling old furniture or purchasing unfinished pieces an attractive alternative.

It is true that restoring a piece of fine wood to its original brilliance or creatively finishing raw furniture can be a painstaking task. But that task can be simplified and made into an enjoyable, creative experience. That is the aim of this book.

(Below) A single coat of polyurethane varnish was used to revive a worn varnish finish on this 1930's style dresser. (Below right) A walk through a cluttered antique shop can help you become aware of furniture that is available for restoration or refinishing.

Selecting Furniture to Work On

Ferreting out the "perfect" piece of furniture to work on can be an intriguing experience. How to look for it will depend on whether you want an authentic antique or simply a piece of pleasing design and function.

The "great antique hunt" of the past decade has greatly limited the choice and availability of fine period furniture. If you are searching for a certain style, say Shaker, see an antique dealer first. Reputable dealers around the country keep their sights on just such premium items. If local dealers fail you, broaden your search. Review library copies of periodicals dealing in antique furniture. Watch local papers for advertisements of auctions and announcements of major antique shows. Familiarize yourself with the market at all levels. Fine reproductions of period furniture are now available from manufacturers of quality unfinished furniture. Send for catalogs and compare.

If you are more interested in design and function than in period and age, you might begin your search at home. Ask family, friends, and neighbors about sources of furniture. Garage sales are a good place to start. Local junk stores, antique shops, second-hand stores, and unfinished furniture outlets are further possibilities. Here the variety and range of choices may be confusing.

In making any purchase, whether it is a new unfinished piece, a second-hand one, or a genuine antique, keep in mind three important considerations: the design, the wood, and the structure.

DESIGN

Usually it is the design of furniture that first strikes the eye. The ability to recognize an interesting design and to visualize how it will look in your own living space can make shopping for used or unfinished furniture a truly creative activity. Be as freewheeling as your budget and imagination allow. This kind of approach can make your living environment a collage of different periods and styles, combining brilliantly painted furniture and finely finished woods.

WOOD

Wood continues to motivate and fascinate artists and craftsmen. They see in its pattern and grain a dynamic expression of the life force as it existed at one instant in time. Trees are taken from the forest, divided, reshaped, and cut into wood and veneers, yet they retain their identity.

Wood, then, concerns us in a unique way. It is largely responsible for creating our environment both inside and out. Chairs, tables, sofas, picture frames, wood paneling, as well as trees on the lawn, are all elements within a total living environment.

Your preference in woods will narrow your search for furniture. Wood is one of the most important considerations in the art of finish-

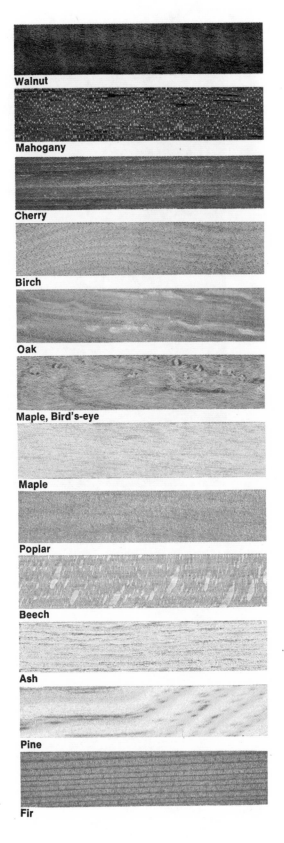

Walnut

Mahogany

Cherry

Birch

Oak

Maple, Bird's-eye

Maple

Poplar

Beech

Ash

Pine

Fir

Fine reproductions of period furniture are now available for finishing at home. (Note the original Shaker chair hanging on the wall.)

ing or refinishing furniture. Do you want a dark wood or a light wood? Do you prefer a painted surface or the look of natural wood? These are matters of personal preference.

When you are out to make a real find in furniture, it is helpful to be familiar with color, figure, and wood classifications. Figure is the pattern of the wood. Grain, the direction of the wood fibers, helps determine figure. Hardwoods and softwoods are classified by their botanical origin, and these terms do not always relate to the actual hardness of the wood. Softwoods are cut from needle-bearing trees, such as evergreens; hardwoods come from broad-leaved, flowering trees. Generally speaking, hardwoods are more desirable for furniture construction because of their internal strength and durability.

The samples showing wood colors and figures on page 5 will give you a start in wood identification. But only a start. They will not make you an expert. Do not be discouraged if you have trouble identifying wood. Many antique dealers who have worked with furniture for years sometimes have difficulty with their identifications. The problem is that trees, like people, are all different. Wood from several trees of the same kind will vary in appearance and may be difficult to recognize.

Here is a simple test anyone can make in identifying the wood in a piece of furniture. First, scrape off some of the finish in an inconspicuous area. If possible, clear about one square inch. Test the exposed wood with a moistened fingertip. This will indicate the actual color of the wood when it is given a clear finish and will aid you in examining the figure. Pore structure is also important in this identification. Walnut, oak, and ash have large, open pores in the grain, while maple and birch have fine, close pores. Other hardwoods illustrated in the samples have medium to fine porosity. Softwoods, such as pine and fir, have no pores and are identified by their texture. Pine is usually more finely textured than fir, and many times can be recognized by the presence of knots.

Keep in mind that scraping one area does not necessarily indicate the composition of the entire piece. Structural considerations often lead furniture designers to use a variety of woods in one piece. Actually, this can sometimes be a plus in your favor. A variety of woods, as well as beautiful inlays, can add real interest to an otherwise static design.

The kind of wood in the furniture you choose should determine the type of finish the furniture is given. Do not discredit a piece of furniture by attempting to disguise the true character of its wood with heavy stains or quick antiquing. If the piece is designed from solid hardwood or antique Eastern pine, preserve the natural beauty with a transparent finish that will allow the wood to show through. Badly damaged hardwoods that are not suitable for transparent finishing can be salvaged with repair and an opaque finish. Some furniture that combines both hardwood and softwood may be visually unacceptable. In this case, an opaque finish was undoubtedly used originally and should be used again.

New, unfinished furniture made of softwoods, generally varieties of pine, is best finished with hard-surface opaque enamels that will beautify as well as protect the soft wood from dents and scratches. Or, if you enjoy the pale look of unfinished furniture, preserve this quality with one of the "nude" transparent finishes.

STRUCTURE

Before you invest your money, time, and energy in a piece of furniture, you should ask, "Is it solid in structure? If damaged, can it be repaired?" Avoid pieces that demand a lot of structural remodeling for your initial project. Regluing and clamping are routine techniques for revitalizing shaky structures, but repair of broken legs, warped tops, and split veneers is best left to experienced furniture workers.

Even though the paint may be chipped and worn, antique painted furniture should not be refinished. The decorated surface of the stenciled arrow-back chair on the left gives it its historic identity, as does the distinctive shade of green on the Shaker sorting table above.

Restoring Furniture

PRESERVING VERSUS REPLACING AN OLD FINISH

The first step in the task of restoring old furniture to its original beauty is to decide what needs to be done. Doing more than necessary can be a mistake. When an old original finish is damaged, there is a tendency to strip it off and replace it with a new finish. But total refinishing such as this can devaluate fine antique furniture. For example, Early American fancy-painted furniture such as Windsors, Boston rockers, landscape medallion chairs, and decorated cabinets lose their historic value when the original painted finish is removed.

Find out whether such painted furniture is authentic before starting to work on it. If it is, have a specialist in the restoration and cleaning of antiques restore the painted finish. He will do this by preserving what remains, not by repainting the original design.

The original paint on plain-painted antique furniture is a valued characteristic of that furniture and should not be removed. The subtle greens, reds, and browns used by the Shakers, Pennsylvania Dutch, and other early craftsmen can never be duplicated. The rustic qualities of this furniture are part of our American heritage, and such pieces are not candidates for refinishing.

To a casual observer, all transparent finishes appear to be similar. But to the antique lover, a clear finish with all its variations from French polish to lacquer tells the history of the furniture. If the original finish is removed, the furniture will lose some of its value as well as its character. Although it continues to be a hotly debated question, the mellow glow of old wood referred to as "patina" is said to be lessened when total refinishing takes place.

A professional restorer should be consulted when the finish of a valuable antique is in question. When dealing with everyday furniture problems, a simple test (below) can be used to determine if refinishing is really necessary.

Testing the old finish. The need for total refinishing is obvious in painted furniture of no historical value. A surface made uneven by chipped paint or blisters, exposing the bare wood, will have to be removed. Transparent finishes do not show their damage as readily.

Test the firmness of a transparent finish by using the edge of a coin. When the surface appears uniform, test in an inconspicuous place. Otherwise, make a test scratch where the strength of the finish is in question. If the coin scrapes easily through the finish and down to the bare wood, or if the pressure of a fingernail can cause the finish to flake, you will want to strip off and replace the finish.

In addition to the coin test, make an aesthetic evaluation. Dark stains and discolored finishes that obliterate beautiful wood figure should also be removed.

Where the finish remains intact and wood figure is clear, begin your restoration with a thorough cleaning.

Testing the old finish with a coin

Cleaning. Enamel, varnish, lacquer, shellac, sealers, and other hard finishes are washable. However, wash your furniture as you would a delicate child. Use mild soap and lukewarm water. Refrain from prolonged scrubbing, but wash until all old wax and grease have been removed. Dry immediately with a soft cloth. A fifty-fifty mixture of turpentine and boiled linseed oil is recommended as a rinse, though it is not mandatory. Rewax or polish when no additional repairs are to be made.

REVIVING DULL TRANSPARENT FINISHES

Shellac, lacquer, and varnish are used as transparent finishes—surface coatings that allow the natural wood to show through. A transparent finish that lacks luster and depth can be restored by using a single coat of the *same* finish as used originally. Shellac or lacquer finishes can sometimes be revived with a coat of varnish, but the reverse is not true. (Never use a varnish—or any other hard finish—over a rubbed oil finish.)

The old finish can be identified by its appearance or by a simple test. Lacquer is easily recognized by its clear glasslike quality and by the fact that it dissolves when rubbed with a cloth dampened in lacquer thinner. Shellac often yellows with age and can be dissolved with denatured alcohol. Gum turpentine will soften a varnish finish.

There are other useful clues to the identity of a finish. The majority of mass-produced American furniture in recent years has been sprayed with lacquer. Old furniture that has never been refinished is likely to have a shellac finish. Varnish is the most popular finish used by home refinishers.

After you discover the identity of the original finish, make sure the furniture is absolutely free of wax and grease. Wash with a trisodium phosphate solution (commonly sold as TSP or sal soda) or a strong detergent dissolved in water. When dry, sand lightly or use a liquid sanding product to degloss the old surface. Then apply a new coat of the original finish (see Transparent Finishing section in the chapter on Final Finishing).

REMOVING SCRATCHES

A deep scratch that has penetrated through a transparent finish into the wood itself can be treated with a colored wax stick in the same manner as nicks, burns, and gouges (see page 12).

Superficial scratches can be filled with dark paste wax, or they can be completely removed by applying the appropriate solvent (see preceding section) to lacquer, shellac, or varnish. When using a solvent, proceed with care. Apply solvent with a thin, pointed brush, painting it along the length of the scratch. As the old finish is dissolved the scratch is filled. Allow this repair to dry completely before attempting to rub out the surface. A final rubbing with powder abrasives and oil or 4/0 steel wool will make the repair invisible.

When using a commercial scratch remover, look for a liquid that hardens and has a brush applicator. Oily scratch removers do not work well on hard transparent finishes.

Applying a wax stick to repair surface nicks and gouges

RAISING DENTS AND DEPRESSIONS

Dents and depressions can be raised by applying water or water and heat to the bare wood. Fill small dents with tepid water and wait for absorption to raise the wood fibers back to the surface. More serious dents and depressions involving large areas of wood can sometimes be raised with steam. To do this, cover the damaged area with a damp woolen cloth and press with a moderately hot iron. Wait for the moisture to be absorbed. After the wood is dry, sand lightly with very fine sandpaper to smooth. It is not advisable to apply water or heat to a finished surface. A clouded finish from water spotting would be more visually disturbing than the dent.

REMOVING RINGS AND WATER SPOTS

White rings caused by cups of steaming liquid or icy drinks can be removed without destroying the finish. The presence of dark rings, however, indicates that moisture has penetrated into the wood below the finish level. These rings can rarely be removed without stripping off the finish.

Many times clouded areas and rings can be removed with a suitable abrasive. When available, pumice mixed with oil is an excellent rubbing compound. Other more common abrasives can also be effective. Table salt, cigar ashes, and steel wool all work well in combination with a lightweight household oil. When using any abrasive, rub only in the direction of the wood grain.

After the spot has been removed, clean the area with mild soap and lukewarm water. Then rub with furniture polish or wax until the abraded area blends into the adjoining surface.

TREATMENT OF CRACKLED OR CRAZED SURFACES

A finish that has been exposed to excessive heat or direct sunlight may develop the fine cracks characteristic of crackled or crazed surfaces. These can usually be corrected easily if the general condition of the finish remains good. Deep cracks and grooves, sometimes called an alligatored finish, are more difficult to remedy.

Prepare the crazed surface by using a mild soap and lukewarm water to clean away all wax. Determine the transparent finish that was originally used (see page 10). Then apply the appropriate solvent to reamalgamate the finish. For shellac, use denatured alcohol. For lacquer, use lacquer thinner. For other finishes, such as varnish, buy a commercial reamalgamating solvent. Use all solvents with caution. Volatile and poisonous, they should be applied only in open air, out of direct sunlight.

Keep the surface to be treated in a horizontal position. If the area to be treated is small, use a soft, tightly woven cloth dampened with solvent. For larger areas, such as an entire table top, use a new, lint-free brush.

Removing a white ring with fine steel wool

Treating a crazed lacquer finish

Proceed with care! Test the power of your solvent and your control in a small area. The task is to liquefy the finish without redistributing it. Don't overbrush. Most brush marks will disappear as the finish dries. If they remain visible, use a rubbing compound or fine steel wool to smooth the surface, then repolish the furniture.

REPAIR OF NICKS, BURNS, AND GOUGES

A general rule for repairing surface damage is that the deeper the injury, the more stable the repair material must be. When surface holes are larger than the circumference of a penny, professional help will be needed. These big repairs require the use of either stick shellac or stick lacquer. Both must be melted and "burned in," and could damage the finish if not properly handled.

Small nicks and gouges can be filled with colored wax sticks available at specialty paint stores.

Before you begin your repair, clean the area thoroughly with mild soap and lukewarm water.

In the case of burns, the hole should be scraped to remove all charred particles. If the wood still remains discolored, bleach with denatured alcohol.

When applying the wax stick, control the flow with a pointed metal rod that has been heated. A nail will do. The molten wax will flow along the rod and into the hole.

Another method is to heat the wax with a smokeless flame (alcohol lamp, sterno) and drip it into the hole. Overfill the depression slightly. Scrape off all excess with a dull knife or small spatula. Pat the repair gently with your fingertips to test for firmness. Unlike shellac or lacquer sticks, wax will give you a second chance if the first attempt at repair fails. Simply scrape it out and start again.

This type of repair will be nearly invisible when the correct color is used. To get the right shade, it may be necessary to melt several colors together.

Seal the repair with shellac after the wax is leveled and dried.

RESTORING PLAIN OPAQUE FINISHES

Enameled finishes are not usually suitable for restoration unless they have antique value. However, a good scrubbing with soap and water will sometimes revitalize painted furniture.

After the surface has been cleaned, check to make sure the finish is enamel. Lacquer has a more crystal-hard appearance and can be dissolved with lacquer thinner.

When an enameled or lacquered surface is in good condition but lacks the glow of a fine finish, use paste wax and buff. This method is recommended for the dark woods of traditional furniture only, since even light paste wax tends to "antique" white or light-colored enamels.

Opaque finishes that show signs of wear or have been chipped or cracked will need to be deglossed, repaired, and recoated with the same opaque finish. (See Opaque Finishing, page 58.)

Removing a scratch with solvent

GLUING LOOSE JOINTS

As a general rule, all techniques for firming structure are more easily accomplished after a piece has been stripped or while it remains in the unfinished state. Nevertheless, a finished piece can be repaired successfully and safely by gluing if special care is taken to protect the finish.

Tools. The tools for gluing are as varied as the jobs they are required to do. The most important are woodworking clamps: "C" clamps, wood clamps, and pipe or bar clamps. When these clamps are not available, use alternatives such as rope tourniquets (see the photograph on page 14), heavy books, or wedge clamps to hold the surfaces together while the glue sets. Gluing furniture without the use of pressure is never successful.

The material. The flexibility that makes wood ideal for furniture tends to present a problem in construction. For this reason, glue has been the principal bonding agent in all fine furniture for centuries. A porous wooden surface that collects moisture and expands, then later dries and contracts, must be held in place without being made rigid. Remember this principle when you are selecting a glue to be used on furniture.

Many waterproof glues tend to be brittle. Epoxy glues are not practical on porous wood surfaces because the bond will not allow the wood to give under stress.

The ideal glue is easy to apply, tough but not brittle, and resistant to water and fungus damage. Although the white household glues are excellent for many purposes, the buff-colored aliphatic resin glue

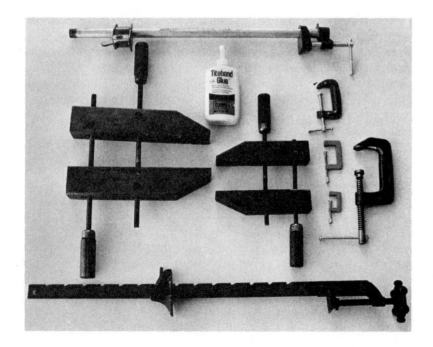

Various clamps used for securing glued furniture include a pipe clamp (top), wood clamps (two sizes), "C" clamps (four sizes), and a bar clamp. Furniture glue is shown at center.

A tourniquet clamp can be used to hold glued structures firm if special clamping tools aren't available.

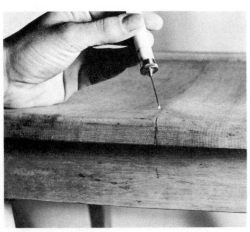

A syringe is a handy tool for injecting glue into hard-to-reach areas.

is superior for bonding wood surfaces. It is available in a squeeze plastic container with a slotted top for easy application.

Preparing the surface. All surfaces that are to be glued must be freed from old glue residue and dirt. Complete dismantling can make this task easier, but is not practical unless the entire structure appears unsound.

Any degree of dismantling should be approached with caution. Remember that the stress of all joints is interdependent, and unequal pressure at any point can cause breakage. Always use a rubber mallet or padded hammer to gently tap joints apart. Firmly glued joints should not be forced. Warm vinegar applications will loosen joints of unfinished or stripped furniture if water-soluble glue has been used.

After joints have been freed, scrape off dried glue with a knife blade. Do not cut into the wood or in any way change the diameter of the piece.

Methods of application. First assemble the furniture and your tools in a warm, dry place. Next, read the suggestions and instructions on the glue bottle or applicator. You will need to know the drying time for the glue in order to plan your gluing procedure properly. All glue should be applied at one time and clamped immediately.

When the wood surfaces to be reassembled are exposed, spread an even coating of glue on all pieces to be joined. For gluing joints and cracks that are impossible to reach with a bottle applicator, fill a clean disposable syringe with glue and insert the needle into the joint. Inject the glue until it begins to overflow.

Even when firm clamping fails to join warped or ill-fitting wood surfaces completely, aliphatic resin glue will fill in small gaps. For this reason, glue must be applied generously. All excess glue can be removed with a damp cloth before or immediately after clamping.

Methods of clamping. Modern wood glues dry quickly, so the clamping method should be planned before gluing begins. After glue is applied and joints reassembled, place the furniture on a level floor and check the alignment.

Hand screw clamps or wood clamps are best for most furniture repair. "C" clamps can be used for small jobs, but should be padded with strips of heavy cardboard to protect the wood from damage. Pipe clamps and bar clamps are good for a variety of big clamping projects. These, too, require padding.

When the correct clamp is not available and cannot be borrowed, the tourniquet method will sometimes supply the pressure you need. To apply the tourniquet, tie heavy cotton clothesline tightly around the area to be clamped, and apply pressure by twisting a wooden dowel inside the rope. This method is particularly effective for encircling furniture legs and spindles, where a number of joints need to be clamped with even pressure in all directions.

Suggested clamping time can be found on the glue manufacturer's label. To be perfectly safe, however, overnight clamping is a good idea.

MINOR STRUCTURAL REPAIRS

It may be difficult to fix a broken piece of furniture correctly without a complete home woodworking shop. Severe breaks and missing pieces call for hand-carved or lathe-turned replacements.

Mending fractures. Fractures along the grain of the wood can be glued in some cases, but usually will not hold properly unless pegged. This is done by drilling a hole at a diagonal to the break, and inserting a wooden pin to strengthen the entire area. Wood screws are not an acceptable method of repairing broken furniture.

Straightening warped wood. Badly warped wood is a product of an uneven or incomplete finish that has allowed moisture to be absorbed on one side, while the other side has remained dry. The wetter side expands while the drier side does not, causing the wood to curve toward the dry side. Warping can often be corrected by allowing moisture to enter the convex side of the wood. Try laying the piece on moist grass or over damp towels near a heat source. When the wood has absorbed enough moisture to return it to its proper shape, replace and secure the wood in its original position. When this is not possible, hold the piece firm with clamps until it is entirely dry. Later, diagnose the reason for warping. Even finishing of both sides and all edges will usually prevent this problem from recurring.

For severe warps and breakage it is always wise to consult an experienced woodworker or furniture repair specialist.

Repairing enlarged joints. Parts of furniture are often joined by fitting one piece tightly into a hole made in a second piece. But after

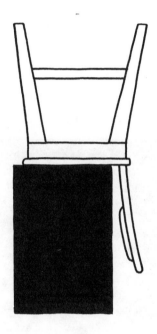

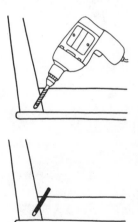

When gluing alone fails to tighten loose joints, a wooden dowel should be inserted. Place furniture on a sturdy table (top picture) and drill as shown. Then coat a ¼-inch dowel with glue and tap into hole.

The period and style of furniture are important considerations for furniture reseating. The three chairs shown here were restored with authentic seating materials that duplicate the materials originally used. The seat and back of the small sewing rocker were recaned, the seat of the handmade Mexican chair was rewoven with fiber cord, and a new splint seat has been woven for the maple rocker.

years of wear, the hole may become enlarged and the pieces fit so poorly that gluing alone will not hold them together.

Several methods of repair are possible. The simplest is to increase the diameter of the inserted piece with cloth. If the joint is rectangular, cut two strips of cloth and place one vertically, the other horizontally, across the end of the piece and along its sides. Round joint ends such as spindles will need only one strip of cloth. Apply glue to both pieces of wood, as well as the cloth, and press the joint together. Cut off excess cloth that remains visible.

Rectangular joints can also be repaired by coating a hardwood shim (thin strip of wood) with glue and then forcing it into the hole to tighten the fit.

Hardwood wedges are another method used to expand rungs, stretchers, and spindles to make them fit tightly inside their corresponding holes or openings. A round or rectangular end must be slotted to allow the piece to accept the wedge. With the wedge in place, glue both ends of the joint as well as the wedge. Locate the wedged piece in the hole and tap into place with a mallet. Chair backs and arms that extend through the wooden seat can be wedged from underneath.

Loose furniture rungs, stretchers, and spindles can be expanded by slotting the loose end and inserting a wedge.

Unsticking drawers. Soap or candle wax applied to drawers and runners will cure minor sticking. When drawers continue to bind, check for loose joints and warp. Joints can be reglued and clamped. Warp can be treated, after the cause of warping has been cured (page 15).

Sticking may also be the result of faulty runners. Runners that are worn down or damaged through use do not allow the drawer to slide properly. To repair, remove each runner and refasten it upside down. Make sure that the runners are level and in the original position. If broken or badly worn, the entire runner may need to be replaced.

Leveling uneven legs. For minor repairs, products such as felt chair pads or metal chair guides are available to lengthen a short leg.

For more serious cases, remove whatever is necessary from the longer legs until all legs are equal. This is particularly difficult when all legs are of varying length. Begin by measuring to determine the real difference between the legs. If the shortest leg is ⅜ of an inch shorter than all the others, cut a block of wood of this size and place it under that leg. Do the same for the next shortest and continue until the piece is level. Using the blocks as your guide, mark the amount to be removed from each leg. Correct any small differences and reshape the newly cut legs with a wood file.

Repairing loose knobs and drawer pulls. Screws holding drawer pulls and knobs tend to loosen over the years. Replacing the original screw with a larger one could in time aggravate the problem. The simplest method of repair is to dip a cotton thread or string (depending upon the size of the screw threads) into liquid glue. Then wrap the wet string around the screw. Before the glue begins to dry, carefully replace the screw in the handle or knob. Wait several hours before using the repaired pull.

Reseating

Cane, rush, and splint are traditional seating materials with a long history of use. They add the interest of texture, as well as offering a pleasant alternative to the costlier and heavier upholstered materials.

Before you begin seat restoration, make all other repairs. When refinishing is necessary, complete before reseating. Cane, rush, and splint are wet weaving processes, making it imperative to have a finish that is in good repair and water resistant.

SEVEN-STEP CANING

Tools. Hardwood pegs, awl, glycerin, small plastic water container, clip clothespins, sponge, towel, drip cloth, scissors or knife.

The material. Cane consists of narrow strips of the outer bark of the rattan palm. (Suppliers are listed on page 80.) It comes in several widths. Determine the width to be used by measuring the size of the holes in the seat frame plus the distance between holes, center to center. Consult the chart on page 19 for the correct size. Cane is purchased in 1-pound bundles that will give you enough material to cane and bind two to four seats. The binding cane is one size larger than the other cane and should be removed and laid aside for later use. Unlike other weaving materials, cane should be pulled through the weaving in the direction that will not snag or damage the "eye." This bump or "eye" on the shiny surface of the cane is where the stem of a leaf once grew from the vine of the rattan palm. You can identify the direction in which each strand slides smoothly by running each strand of cane between your fingers before inserting it into the weaving.

To begin. First, make sure all edges of the furniture frame are rounded so they will not damage the new cane seat. If the inside edge of a seat frame is sharp, round it slightly with a wood file or sander.

Each caning project is different and needs individual consideration. For instance, a large caned area, such as the rocker back or the seat of the bentwood settee below, requires less tension than a smaller area, such as a regular chair seat. When caning large areas, keep weaving tension loose during the first three steps.

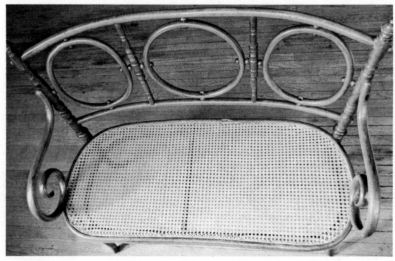

Pull a single strand of cane from the looped end of the bundle. Try to choose a long strand. Wrap this strand around your fingers, shiny side out, to form a coil small enough to fit in the water container. Secure it with a clothespin. To moisten the cane, prepare a glycerin solution using 10 percent glycerin or approximately 1½ tablespoons per cup of water. Make enough solution to totally cover several coils of cane. Submerge the cane in the solution for 10 minutes (20 minutes at the maximum). Add a second coil of cane to the solution after the first coil has been removed.

TO DETERMINE SIZE OF CANE

To determine the correct size of cane to use, first measure the size of a single hole. Next, measure the distance between two holes, center to center. When the distance between holes varies, estimate an average. Consult chart below.

Cane Widths	Size of Hole in Seat	Distance Center to Center
Common	⁵⁄₁₆''	⅞''
Medium	¼''	¾''
Fine	³⁄₁₆''	⅝''
Fine Fine	³⁄₁₆''	½''
Superfine	³⁄₁₆''	⅜''
Carriagefine	⅛''	⅜''

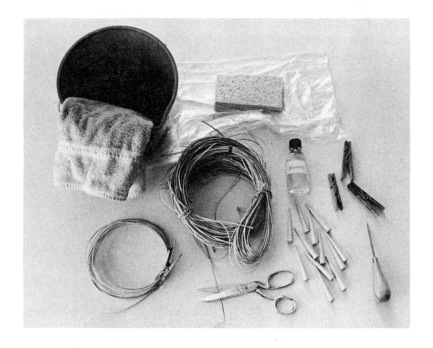

Tools for caning include a water container, towel, plastic drip cloth, sponge, glycerin, clothespins, awl, pegs, scissors, weaving cane (above), and binding cane (left).

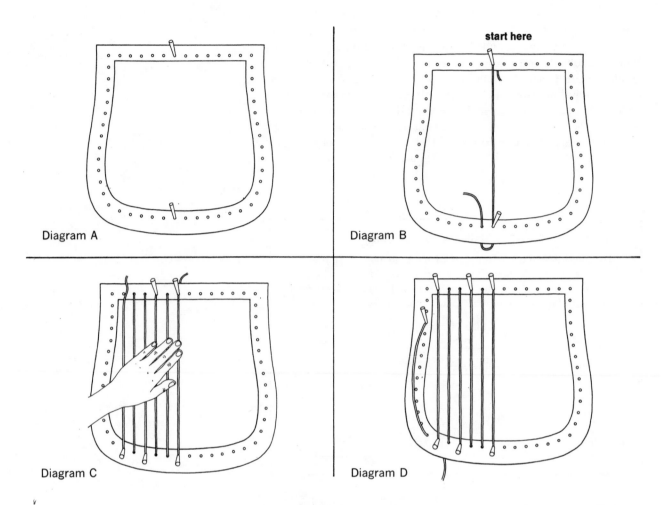

Diagram A

start here

Diagram B

Diagram C

Diagram D

Step 1: Count the holes in the back frame of the seat. Find the center hole (or left center hole if there are an even number of holes) and mark with a peg. Likewise, mark the center hole (or left center hole) in the front of the frame with a peg (diagram A). Remove the back peg and push the first strand of moistened cane through the hole until the cane extends about 3 inches below the frame. Repeg to hold in place. Pull this strand of cane straight (not taut) across to the center front hole, remove the peg, feed the cane through this hole, and repeg. Working under the front frame, feed the cane up through the first hole to your left and peg (diagram B). Then go across to the first hole to the left in the back. Continue working in this same manner, leaving an even amount of slack in all the strands (diagram C). For curved seats, such as the one in the diagram, separate pieces of cane must be inserted at either side (diagram D).

After completing the left half, work on the right. When it is necessary to add new strands of cane, tie to existing cane underneath the frame. Make sure both pieces of cane are moist before tying. Tie the end of each strand to a loop of cane with a half hitch (diagram E), or tie the two ends together with a square knot. Do not cut the excess from the knots until the cane is perfectly dry.

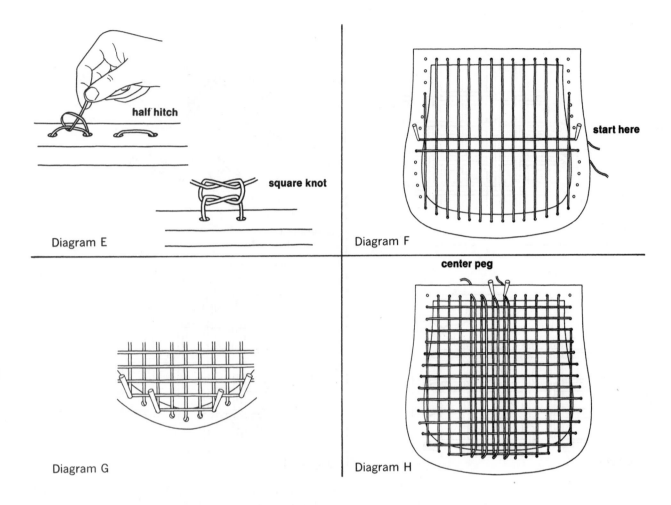

Diagram E

square knot

half hitch

Diagram F

start here

center peg

Diagram G

Diagram H

Step 2: Locate the center hole (or left center hole) in each side frame and peg. Insert a strand into the center hole of the right-hand side of the frame. Peg and pull across Step 1 strands to the opposite center peg. Remove peg, feed cane through the hole and repeg (diagram F). Test for moderate tension of the cane with the flat of your hand. Continue to add caning, working toward the front frame. In the case of a curved front frame, use separate pieces of cane as in the sides (diagram G). When the front half of the seat is complete, go back to the center and add cane to the back half.

Step 3: This is a repetition of Step 1, but begin caning one hole to the right of the center peg in the back frame. Follow the procedure described for Step 1, the only difference being that each strand in the sequence is to the right of the corresponding strand in Step 1 (see diagram H)

Step 4: Actual weaving now begins. Find the center hole in the right-hand frame used for Step 2. Come forward one hole, place a new strand of cane into this hole, and peg. Dampen all surfaces of cane about to be woven. Do this by placing a moist towel across the warped cane before the weaving begins.

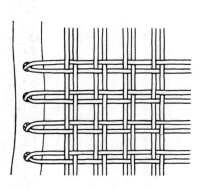

Diagram I

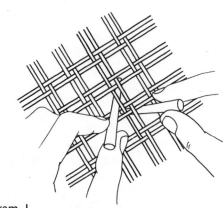

Diagram J

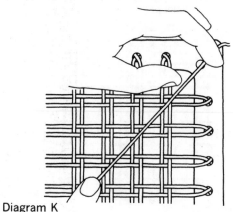

Diagram K

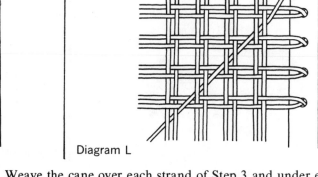

Diagram L

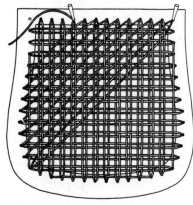

Diagram M

Weave the cane over each strand of Step 3 and under each strand of Step 1. Keep the weaving strand damp by pulling it through a wet towel or sponge. Complete this section, working toward the front frame (diagram I). Then weave the back section. Make sure the woven cane forms a pattern of perfect squares. Place a yardstick over caning as a guide and straighten the moistened rows. Force them together using the hardwood pegs (diagram J).

Step 5: To begin diagonal weaving, find the back hole at the right-hand corner of the frame (diagram K). Peg the cane and lay it across your work in a straight diagonal to the corresponding front hole. Mark this hole with a peg. Use this peg as a marker as you begin to weave forward from the back corner. To form this diagonal, weave cane over the pairs formed by Steps 2 and 4 and under the pairs formed by Steps 1 and 3 (diagram L). Use one hand underneath the work to assist in sliding the cane over and under the woven squares. Weave only a few pairs at a time before pulling the entire strand through. Keep strand on a parallel plane with weaving; do not pull above weaving level. Check for mistakes frequently. Weaving is incorrect when cane binds against the woven square. Diagonal strands should pull easily when moist. Lay a damp towel over weaving area and pull the strand through the towel.

Continue to weave diagonals, working toward the back section of the frame. Before each row is woven, check to determine its corresponding hole on the opposite side of the frame (diagram M). It will sometimes be necessary to use the same hole twice to keep the rows straight. This often happens with the corner holes, front and back. Here, two strands entering the same hole from different woven rows will form a "V" known as a fish head (diagram N).

The awl will be needed in Step 5 to clear holes before additional cane can be added. Always insert the awl slowly to avoid splitting cane already in the holes. Complete the front triangle of the frame in the same manner as the back. Tie loose strands underneath the frame as you work.

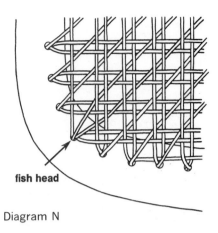

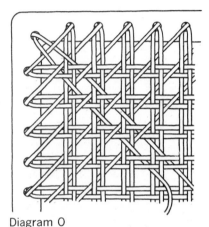

Diagram N

Step 6: Start at the back hole in the left-hand side of the frame. Weave over the pairs formed by Steps 1 and 3 and under the pairs of Steps 2 and 4 (diagram O). This procedure is exactly the opposite of Step 5. Fill the front triangular section of the seat with diagonal rows of weaving first. Then progress to the back section. As in Step 5, fish heads will be necessary for weaving corner holes.

Before the final step, make sure all cane is tied and cut underneath the frame. Check to see that there are no mistakes in weaving and that the seat is formed from evenly shaped hexagonals. Correct any errors. Make the pattern of holes more uniform by dampening the cane and inserting a pencil or peg (diagram P). The hairlike projections caused by shedding cane should be clipped off to make the entire woven surface smooth to the touch.

Diagram O

Step 7: First, make sure you are using the binding cane, which is wider than the weaving cane. Measure the amount of binding needed by placing the cane over the holes around the circumference of the frame. Allow an overlap of two or three holes. Most seats have curved corners and can be bound with one continuous piece of cane.

Wind and soak the measured strand of binding, as well as a strand of weaving cane, for approximately 15 minutes. The binding will not follow the curves of the seat without being thoroughly moist.

Insert the binding cane in the left-hand corner hole at the back. Peg temporarily to hold in place. Lay the binding over the holes in the back of the frame. Tie the moist strand of regular weaving cane under the frame and bring it up through the next hole to the right. Now begin to secure the binding by weaving the regular cane up and over the binding and down through the same hole (diagram Q), then over and up through the next hole. Pull these loops tight, both on the surface of the chair and underneath. Be sure the binding is centered over the holes as you continue. Any slack left in the weaving cane will allow the binding to slip. Moisten cane and binding again when turning corners. Finally, overlap the binding material for at least two holes, carefully sliding the end of the binding under the section previously bound. Clip off the binding next to a loop formed by the regular cane to make the splice invisible. The woven loops should now be flattened before they are allowed to dry. Do this by tapping each loop with the flat, wooden end of the awl.

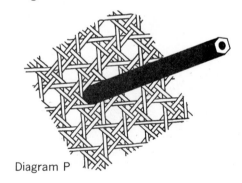

Diagram P

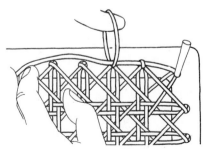

Diagram Q

REPLACING PREWOVEN OR PRESSED CANE

Tools. Five or more hardwood wedges, rubber mallet, water-soluble glue, utility knife, 1-inch flat-bladed chisel, 3/32-inch sharp chisel, glycerin, water container, towel, scissors.

The material. Prewoven or pressed cane needs no weaving. It can be replaced in one piece. It is fastened by inserting and gluing it in a groove extending around the opening. A thin strip of reed called a spline fits into the opening over the cane, helping to hold it in place.

Cane webbing comes in two different styles—open and close weave. The open weave is available in four different sizes from superfine, a ⅜-inch mesh, to medium, a ⅝-inch mesh. It is possible to buy webbing in varying widths, ranging from 12 inches to a maximum of 24 inches. The length is sold by the running foot and will depend upon the size of the seat you wish to restore. (Suppliers are listed on page 80.)

To determine the amount of webbing needed, measure the width and length of the seat from groove to groove. For safety, add 1 inch or more in all directions. The material must overlap the groove on all sides in order to be installed properly.

To determine the length of spline needed, measure the old spline or the groove it fit in and add 4 inches. If you are ordering material without specific catalog sizes, send samples of the old webbing and spline along with your measurements.

When you are uncertain about the original material, look through books that feature similar furniture to determine the mesh size and

Tools for pressed cane seating include a water container, towel, utility knife, glue, wedges, chisels, scissors, mallet, glycerin, prewoven cane (two types are pictured), and a length of spline.

style of cane that is appropriate for your piece. You will then need to consult a supplier's catalog for cane and spline measurements.

To begin. Remove the old reed spline from its groove, using chisels. The old spline is dispensable, but the wood surrounding it is not. The two chisels mentioned in "Tools" were especially designed for this job. The 3/32-inch chisel will chip away sections of the old spline, while the larger, flat-bladed chisel will assist in separating the spline from the edge of the seat frame. You may substitute other tools, such as a screwdriver, at your own risk.

After the spline and damaged webbing are removed, scrape the groove to clean away all old glue and cane particles.

The first step is to establish the general dimensions of the replacement piece. When replacing large areas, such as a chair back, make a paper pattern of the opening, overlapping the groove 1 inch or so in all directions (photo A). Lay the new webbing flat, place the pattern on top with all lines of the webbing parallel to the sides or front of the pattern, and cut out the correct-size replacement piece with scissors.

For smaller jobs, place the actual flattened webbing over the open area. Make sure all rows of cane are parallel to the sides or front of the opening. Hold the webbing in place with one hand and cut with scissors. Now measure the length of the groove. A curved groove will require a single piece of reed. Apply pressure with the fingers and fit the spline loosely into the groove. Allow 1 inch overlap and cut off extra material.

Grooves with squared corners require several pieces of spline. To fit each piece, insert it loosely in a groove, mark at the corners, and remove and cut. Bevel the ends of adjoining pieces so they form a mitered joint where they meet.

Submerge the spline in tepid water for two minutes. Then wrap it in a towel and lay it aside.

Prepare a glycerin solution (1½ tablespoons of glycerin to 1 cup of water) in a container large enough to totally submerge cane webbing. Soak the webbing until it becomes pliable—but do not soak over 20 minutes, or the cane may darken.

Spread a fine line of water-soluble glue inside the groove. Remove the cane from the water and place it over the opening, with all lines parallel to the front or the sides. Now insert the first two hardwood wedges. Use the rubber mallet to drive the wedges and webbing into the groove—one at the back of the opening, another at the front. Leave wedges in place. Then drive two more wedges into place, one at the center of each side (photo B). Leave all four wedges in place. Additional wedges are now inserted and removed to force webbing into the groove around the entire opening. If there are corners, leave them until last. Special care must be taken to prevent the woven cane from separating at these points.

Make sure all cane ends are properly inserted into the groove. Use a sharp utility knife or chisel to cut off excess cane slightly below the top of the groove (photo C, page 26).

A. Check to make sure paper pattern overlaps groove approximately 1 inch in all directions.

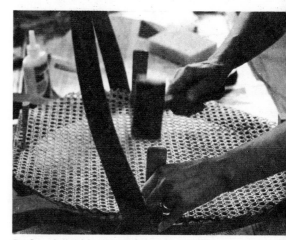

B. Carefully drive cane into place with mallet and hardwood wedges.

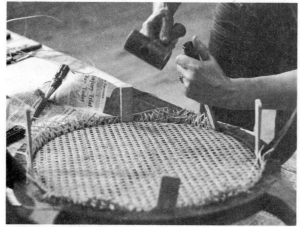

C. Cut off excess cane just below top of groove.

D. Squeeze a thin line of glue inside groove.

E. Drive spline into groove with mallet and hardwood wedge.

F. After measuring, cut off excess spline length.

Facing page: The replacement of a rectangular area of prewoven cane, as in this carved armchair styled after 17th-century Charles II chairs, requires four separate sections of spline, each with a mitered corner.

Apply another thin line of water-soluble glue inside the groove, on top of the pressed cane. Spread evenly with a toothpick or piece of cane (photo D).

Remove spline from towel. To insert a spline that will remain in a single piece, begin at a point in the groove where the seam will be least noticeable.

Apply pressure with the fingers until the spline fits loosely in the groove. Tap the spline down into the groove using the flat side of a hardwood wedge and the rubber mallet (photo E). Just before the final section is tapped into place, cut off any excess length (photo F).

Before pressing adjoining pieces of spline into a groove with squared corners, insert them loosely to be sure the mitered corners are correct. Then tap each piece of spline into the groove using a wedge and mallet as described.

RUSH SEATING

Tools. Sharp knife or scissors, bucket, masking tape, towel, large spring clamp, rubber mallet, a wedge or small wooden block, large carpenter's square, transparent sealer, thick brush.

The material. Authentic rush seating was woven from reedlike leaves of the cattail plant. These leaves were gathered, tied in loose bundles, and dried. Later, they were soaked and twisted into weaving material.

Today, fiber cord is available. It is easier to use and more practical for furniture. However, in special cases, when a valuable antique chair is to be restored, the original material should be duplicated.

Before making this decision, examine the original seating. When portions of the material remain, it is simple to distinguish fiber cord from natural rush. Turn the chair over. Old rush seating appears irregular, while fiber cord has an even appearance top and bottom.

If the seating frame is totally bare, your only clue to the original weaving material will be the design of the chair. It is possible that neither natural nor fiber rush was used. High, ornate ladder-back chairs did have rush seats, while lower, country-style chairs were woven with splint. More decorative styles of furniture always call for rush seating, and squared corner posts are a definite indication that some type of rush should be used.

The amount of material needed will depend upon the size of the seat opening. Two pounds of fiber cord will rush a small to average chair. Two pounds of natural leaf rush will weave a seat 14 inches by 14 inches.

If the fiber cord seat is stuffed properly as weaving progresses (see page 30), the finished seat will be even and firm.

Tools for rush seating include a water container, towel, sealer, brush, utility knife, wedge, mallet, masking tape, spring clamp, fiber cord, and a carpenter's square.

Fiber rush is available in different colors and sizes. The most commonly used cord is light brown and 6/32 inch in size. It is sold by the single pound or in 35- to 40-pound reels. (Suppliers are listed on page 80.)

Cured natural rush is also sold by the pound, but if you enjoy doing things the natural way, cut and cure your own cattail rush. It is advisable to have prior experience with fiber-cord weaving, since each reed of natural rush must be soaked, twisted, and joined, complicating the weaving process.

To begin. Fiber cord should never be *soaked* in water. To make it more pliable, plunge a working portion (usually ½ pound or less) into tepid water, remove, and wrap in a towel.

To make the material easier to handle, bundle a working portion into a figure eight and secure with a rubber band so that it "feeds" properly as weaving progresses. Another method for meticulous weavers is to place a coil of material in a plastic bag and secure the weaving cord with a rubber band so it can be pulled out as needed.

Oblong or irregular seats. Most chair seats are wider at the front than at the back. As a result, the seat opening is irregular in shape. To compensate for this, single strands of rush have to be woven in such a way that they make the opening into a rectangle. At this point regular rush weaving can begin.

First, use a carpenter's square to determine the points on the front rail that are opposite the ends of the back rail. Mark these two points with tape. The end of the back rail, the mark on the front rail, and the end of the front rail will form a triangle of space on each side, as shown in diagram A. Your first job will be to fill these triangles with rush. Begin by cutting a cord that is 1½ times as long as the front rail. Tape the end of the cord inside the left-hand rail, about 3 inches back from the front post. Weave this cord over and under the front rail, up and over itself, and over and under the left-hand rail. Pull the cord from under the left-hand rail across the length of the front rail. Now go over and under the right-hand rail, over the cord, and over and under the front rail. Tape the end of this cord to the inside of the right-hand rail (diagram B). Cut off any extra cord.

Add a second cord in the same manner, but tape it slightly behind the first cord on the left-hand rail. Keep adding single cords until you have filled the front corners and reached the tape marks on the front rail (diagram C). Continue as directed for square or rectangular seats.

Square or rectangular seats. Dampen and bundle a working portion of cord. Begin at the left-hand side of the chair. Secure the free end of the cord to the inside of the left-hand rail. It should be taped about 3 inches back from the front post, or in the case of irregular seats, behind the last single weaving cord. The weaving cord will first go over and under the front rail, over itself, and over and under the left-hand rail. (Follow diagram D.) Pull taut, taking the cord straight across to the right-hand rail. Go over and under the right-hand rail, over the cord, and over and under the front rail. Pull tight and follow the length

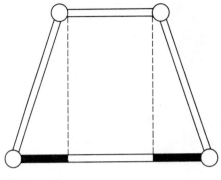

Diagram A

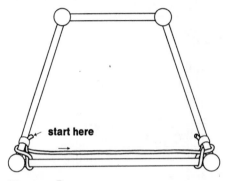

Diagram B

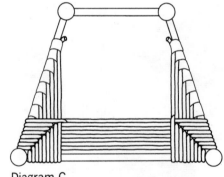

Diagram C

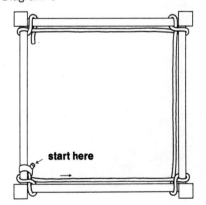

Diagram D

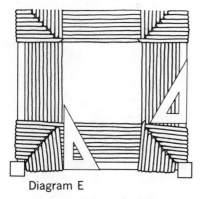

Diagram E

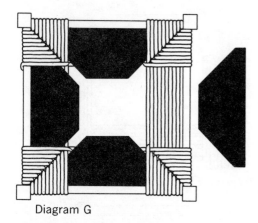

Diagram F

Diagram G

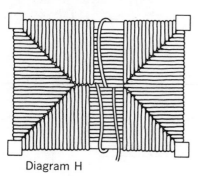

Diagram H

of the side until you reach the back. Weave over and under the back rail, over the cord, and over and under the right-hand rail. Pull tight and follow the length of the back. Go over and under the left-hand rail, over the cord, and over and under the back rail. Pull tight and follow the length of the left rail. Continue to repeat this procedure.

Do not allow the cord to twist. Pull the cord tight and hold it taut as you weave. Remember that each corner will be woven opposite from the one just completed.

Make invisible splices to the fiber cord inside the seat where the cord runs parallel with the rails. The cord can be tied with a square knot or spliced with masking tape that is wrapped and tied with a string. After two cords are spliced, turn them so they will become less visible and fit in between the rows of cord.

As the weaving progresses, the cord will begin to build up a pattern forming a square around each corner post. This weaving pattern should also form a diagonal line, beginning at the inside corner of each post. Check periodically to make sure the four squares remain equal. (Oblong seats will not be equal front and back.) Use a triangle or square to check their size (diagram E). Any differences evident in the squares of weaving can be corrected by closing the space between fiber cords. This is accomplished by forcing the cord together. Place a wooden block or wedge against the cord along the railing and tap with a rubber mallet (diagram F). After all cords are pressed tightly together, apply a large spring clamp to hold them in place as weaving continues.

After three or four inches of weaving have been completed, cut corrugated cardboard triangles and insert into the woven rush (diagram G). This padding controls the shape and firmness of the final seat. Additional padding will be needed as the seat takes shape.

Brown kraft paper, such as lightweight paper bags, can be used to firm the woven pattern. Tear the paper into pieces, sprinkle with water, and crumple slightly before inserting into the pockets formed by the weaving. Use a flat-handled salad spoon as a stuffer. Stuff the seat as weaving progresses and continue to pound the rush with a wedge and mallet to insure a snug fit around the rails.

Most seating frames are not perfectly square. The side rails will be filled with cord before the front and back rails. Complete the open center section by forming a figure eight. Go over and around the front rail and up through the center. Then go over and around the back rail and up through the center (diagram H). Repeat this procedure until back and front rails are tightly filled with cord. Secure the cord end inside the woven seat.

Fiber-cord seats require finishing to make them more attractive and durable. Use a transparent tung-oil sealer that will penetrate into the twisted paper cord and prevent it from stretching or fraying. Several coats will be necessary. Recoat and dry until the fiber-cord surface has darkened into an even finish.

SPLINT SEATING

Tools. Sharp knife or scissors, bucket, masking tape, sponge, glycerin, strong string or thread, clip clothespins, carpenter's square, transparent sealer, thick brush.

The material. Although splint is less common than rush seating, it exemplifies American craftsmanship. Originally, splint woven into seats for country-style furniture was hand cut from the inner bark of hickory and ash trees. Now, only a few Appalachian craftsmen continue the tradition of soaking and splitting the bark from hickory logs. Most weaving splint is machine cut.

Machine-cut ash splint can be purchased by the pound. It is available in three different widths: ½ inch, ⅝ inch, and ¾ inch. The most commonly used width, the ⅝ inch, can be expected to weave an average seat measuring approximately 15 inches across the front. (Suppliers are listed on page 80.)

To begin. Pull a long, straight piece of splint from the bundle and inspect it for flaws. One side of the splint will appear smooth compared to the opposite side, which will be filled with splintery material. Run your fingers along the length of the splint to check for breakage or cracks. Also, note the grain. The direction of the grain will become important when weaving begins. Splint slides easily through the warpers when working in the direction of the grain. Now roll the splint, smooth side out, clip with a clothespin, and submerge for 30 minutes or so in a solution of 1½ tablespoons of glycerin to a cup of water. Soak several strands at one time, replacing each with another as it is used.

If the front rail of the chair seat is longer than the rear rail, use a carpenter's square to mark off the excess length at each end of the front rail. The center section of the seat will be filled with splint first.

Now you are ready to start warping—that is, wrapping the splint lengthwise around front and back rails. Remove a damp strand of splint from the water. Tie or tape it inside the left-hand rail with the rough side of the splint facing out and the short end pointing forward. Next, take the splint under, then up and over, the back rail, positioning it next to the left back post. Pull the strand across the seat opening and around the front rail to the right of the measured mark (diagram A). Pass the splint strand under the seat rails and up and over the back rail. Continue this warping until the back rail is filled with splint. Do not pull the splint taut. Allow even give in each round, or warper, to provide room for weaving. However, do not allow space between the warpers. They must run parallel and fit together as closely as possible.

Add another splint by splicing it to the end of the original warper. Place the new piece over the end of the old and cut small indentations in both. Tie with a strong thread or string (diagram B). These indentations will hold the spliced pieces together without slipping. Always splice the splint under the seat where it will not be evident.

When you have filled the back rail, you will also have filled the

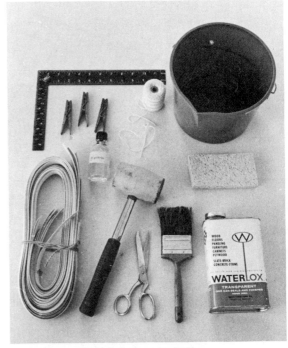

Tools for splint weaving include a water container, sponge, sealer, brush, scissors, mallet, string, carpenter's square, clothespins, glycerin, and splint.

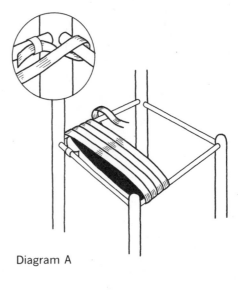

Diagram A

Diagram B

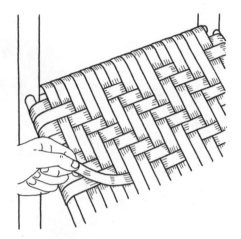

Diagram C

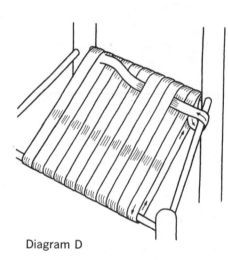

Diagram D

Several coats of tung oil (or other transparent sealer) are required to produce an even sheen on the finished splint seat.

front rail if both rails are of equal length. If the front rail is longer, you will have reached the mark previously made on the right side of the front rail. In either case, secure the loose warp strand under the seat with a clothespin.

You are now ready to consider your weaving pattern. If there was no indication of the original pattern, review several possibilities. The twill pattern is most commonly used for splint weaving. It is a simple pattern of 2 over, 2 under or 2 over, 3 under (as here), but it acquires its distinctive zigzag design from advancing the pattern one warp as each new row is woven (diagram C). The size of the seat opening and the width of the splint will influence your final weave. The larger the seat and the smaller the splint, the more varied the twill combinations may be. For example, a pattern that goes under or over 4 or 5 warpers would be feasible for weaving a large seat with narrow splint.

If you have had no previous weaving experience of any kind, test your design by constructing a paper pattern. Use two separate colors for the warpers and the weavers. (The warpers run "vertically," or front to back, and the weavers run "horizontally," or crosswise, filling the warp.) More experienced weavers who plan an elaborate design may prefer to draw the weaving pattern on graph paper to check its balance, harmony, and practicality before weaving begins.

Now that you are ready to weave, sponge the warp top and bottom until the splint is thoroughly damp and pliable. Find the loose warper held with the clothespin. Splice another strand to the end midway along the bottom of the seat. Bring the new strand around the back rail, and around and over the right-hand rail. The warper has now become the weaver! (See diagram D.)

Begin your weaving pattern as close to the back post as possible. Continue weaving across the top of the chair until you reach the left-hand rail. Check for mistakes after every row of weaving. Don't worry if your pattern does not follow a perfect sequence at the side rails. Go around the side rail and continue the pattern on the bottom of the seat. Turn the chair upside down and place on a table to make weaving more convenient.

New weaving strands can be attached as previously shown, or can be overlapped so they will not pull loose. When adding weaving strands, check the splint grain. When the grain is not obvious, try both ends of the strand to determine which end slides through the weaving more easily.

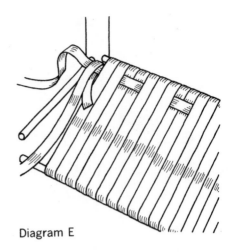

Diagram E

If the chair frame becomes larger toward the front, the weaving strand directly in front of the back posts will need support. At this point, add a single warper at either side of the seat. Remove a strand of splint from the water and crease it several inches back from the end. Insert this over the weaver (diagram E). The other end will cross around and under the front rail and meet itself under the seat, to be spliced and tied.

Continue weaving in the same manner, adding warpers as the need arises (diagram F). Generally, no more than four warpers will be needed to complete the front rail.

Stuff the splint seat in the same manner recommended for rush seats (page 30). Although stuffing is not mandatory, it will produce a firmer, better-wearing seat. Use plain newsprint paper or any other light-colored pliable paper that will pack when moist and hold the seat firm. Seat stuffing is done while the weaving is in progress.

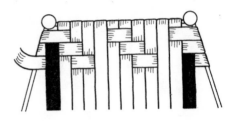

Diagram F

Remember to keep the splint moist during the entire weaving process. Dry splint will break and splinter. After you have completed a row of weaving, straighten the warp and press the warpers together to keep them parallel.

The final row of weaving will be difficult because the previous weaving will have tightened the warp and because the front rail will lie just beneath your weaving area. To assist in weaving, insert the handle of a flat-handled teaspoon under the warper and slide the weaver up through the open area (diagram G). The last weaver will curve slightly toward the front as it holds the warpers tightly along the front rail of the chair.

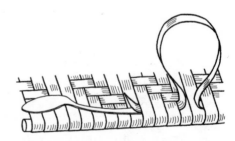

Diagram G

As the woven seat begins to dry, trim off splinters and loose materials to smooth the surface. Splint seats can be left bare, but in most cases it is more practical to seal the freshly woven seat with transparent tung oil. After the splint is dry, apply sealer to both top and bottom. Several coats will seal out moisture and dirt. Dry each coat completely before the next is applied.

When choosing painted furniture to refinish, remember that layers of old paint are most easily removed from fine-grained woods, while porous, unsealed woods usually retain paint residue even after the finish has been removed. An example of successful paint removal is shown in these before and after photos of a fine-grained maple chair.

Removing the Finish

STRIPPING

In spite of the advertising claims made by manufacturers of paint and varnish removers, stripping the finish off of furniture still remains a difficult task. Few people really enjoy this part of refinishing, yet it is a necessary step to insure the success of the final product.

To make stripping less harrowing, become familiar with the finish you wish to remove.

If the finish is transparent, you may be able to recognize a lacquer finish by its glasslike look or an old shellac finish by its often yellowish appearance. Varnish has neither of these characteristics. The identification can be clinched by testing a small area with appropriate solvents. Lacquer is dissolved by lacquer thinner, shellac by denatured alcohol, and varnish by gum turpentine.

The correct solvent can be used to remove a lacquer or shellac finish, while varnish and other transparent finishes should be removed with a commercial paint and varnish remover.

Deal with paint in the same manner as varnish. A semi-paste paint and varnish remover that is nonflammable and water soluble will usually do the best job.

Tools. #2 steel wool, Popsickle sticks, old stiff paintbrush, soft wire brush, cotton cord, drip pan, metal container, masking tape, newspapers, goggles, rubber gloves.

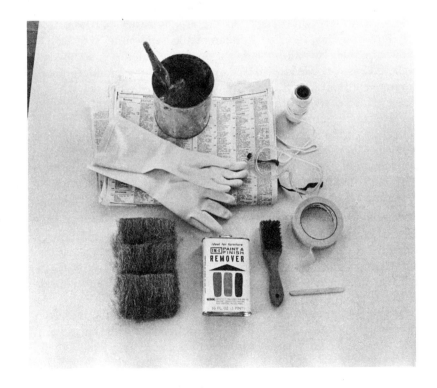

Tools for stripping include an old paintbrush, metal container, newspapers, cotton cord, goggles, masking tape, Popsickle stick, wire brush, solvent or remover, steel wool, and rubber gloves.

The material. Solvents such as lacquer thinner and denatured alcohol which remove lacquer and shellac (respectively) are inexpensive and readily available. However, follow all label precautions since both solvents are highly flammable and poisonous if used in an unventilated area. Commercial paint and varnish removers are available at a variety of prices and in different consistencies. These mixtures range from the highly dangerous flammable and poisonous liquids to the non-flammable, less poisonous semi-pastes.

When buying strippers for any purpose, read the label for contents first. Beware of those containing benzol or benzene. These chemicals are hazardous to inhale or to get on the skin.

Other removers that warn "highly flammable" are so volatile that the slightest spark can cause a flash fire. Less flammable products are now being produced that dominate the market. Although they eliminate the hazards of flash fires, they can become dangerous when exposed to extreme heat. Pressures may build in overheated containers, and noxious gases may be produced.

In the final analysis, no chemical solvent is totally safe and non-toxic. Because of the nature of the job these solvents are required to do, all must contain harmful chemicals.

After all factors are considered, nonflammable semi-paste removers are your best and safest buy. Because of the paste consistency, they are easier to apply. They stay on the surface without dripping or running, and they evaporate less quickly than liquids.

Semi-paste removers are available in two different types—those that are soluble in, and can be washed off with, water; and those that require scraping followed by mineral spirits cleanup. Use non-water-soluble removers for delicate furniture, veneers, or very old pieces. Otherwise, water-soluble removers are usually easier and faster.

Before you buy the first nonflammable semi-paste you see, be knowledgeable. Not all of these products are equally good. Even a high price will not assure you of quality—or of the product's ability to remove all finishes. It is possible that some removers will discolor wood, retard drying of the new finish, or transfer paint pigments to the bare wood grain.

Because of the number of products on the market and the variety of finishes they are required to remove, recommending a single brand becomes impossible. If you would rather not experiment, consult a consumers' magazine. The performance rating of these products will indicate the safest, hardest-working stripper for your particular job.

Preparation. Remove all hardware, knobs, and pulls. Clean or strip these separately as necessary. Plug screw holes and keyholes in all drawers with paper. Drawers should be removed and stood on end so that the surface to be stripped is horizontal. To avoid extra clean-up, mask off the inside of drawers with newspaper fastened by masking tape.

Dismantle furniture when it is held together by screws, such as a bureau with a framed mirror, or a corner cupboard with top and bottom sections. Remove mirrors from frames before stripping.

Careful preparation and a well-planned work space will make any stripping job easier.

If furniture has been glued, be sure the glue is totally dry and firm before stripping is begun.

Prepare your work area properly. When working indoors, cover all surfaces that might be damaged by the remover. Work in an area where fumes of the stripping compound will be carried away by a ventilation fan or through an open door or window. Low furniture can be more easily stripped if placed on a covered table or workbench. Other furniture should be placed on the floor after it is protected by layers of newspaper or a drip pan.

When working outside, stay out of direct sunlight. Position your work so that the wind will carry fumes away from you. Protect your skin by wearing rubber gloves (not plastic) and old clothing. Protect your eyes with sunglasses or goggles.

Where only partial stripping is necessary, mask off all other areas with heavy layers of newspaper secured by paper tape.

Do not pour remover into plastic containers since it may dissolve them. For the same reason, use brushes with wooden rather than plastic handles.

To begin. Read the instructions on the container of paint and varnish remover or solvent. Shake if so directed. Cover the container with a cloth and remove the cap slowly, allowing all pressure to escape. Pour a small amount of the solvent or remover into a metal container.

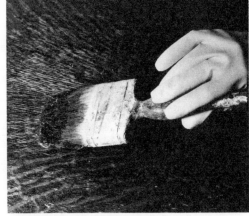

When using varnish remover, flow a thick coating onto the surface to be stripped.

Lacquer and shellac finishes can usually be removed quickly without mess. Both lacquer thinner and denatured alcohol can be brushed on the surface or flooded on with steel wool, causing the old finish to dissolve. The residue can then be removed by rubbing with a clean cloth. When several coats of finish are present, several applications of solvent will be necessary.

When you encounter a particularly tough shellac finish, mix a solvent that contains ⅔ denatured alcohol and ⅓ lacquer thinner. For a tough lacquer finish, reverse the proportions—⅔ lacquer thinner to ⅓ denatured alcohol. Do not store these combinations. Use them immediately and discard.

When using a paint and varnish remover, saturate a brush with the remover and flow it on the surface to be stripped. If the remover begins to dry before it has dissolved or softened the finish, apply a heavier coat in the same direction. Do not brush back and forth as in painting, but allow stripper to accumulate on the surface.

Most removers work within 15 to 20 minutes. The longer a moist solvent stays on the surface the better the stripping action. But do not allow the stripper to dry. Concentrate your efforts on one section at a time.

For water-soluble strippers, prepare a wash-off solution of cold water and sal soda (TSP) or strong detergent (about 2 quarts water to 1 cup cleaner). For non-water-soluble strippers, use mineral spirits as the washing solution. When many layers of paint are to be removed, you may need two grades of steel wool. Begin the stripping operation with #3 steel wool for heavily caked paint; otherwise, use #2 grade.

Dip the steel wool pad into the washing solution until it is thor-

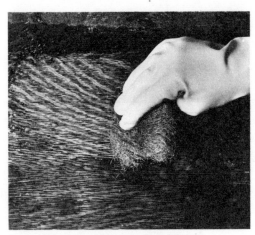

Once stripping action is complete, remove the sludge with a steel wool pad dipped in a TSP solution.

oughly saturated. Rub off the old finish. Be careful to work with the wood grain when it is apparent. For intricate carving, wet a small steel-bristled brush or a coarse, natural-bristled brush and scrub gently. To clean the type of turnings found in spool furniture, use cotton cord dipped into the washing solution. If the stripper has not penetrated into the crevices of the spool, use a cord dipped in stripper first. When scraping is necessary, use the side of a Popsickle stick or heavy cardboard. A sharpened Popsickle stick or cotton swab wrapped with steel wool will clean hard-to-reach corners. Avoid any type of metal scraper that might gouge and scratch the wood after it has been softened by the action of the stripper.

When a patch or a newly turned piece of wood has been added to the furniture, make sure the sludge from the stripping action carries onto the new wood. This will stain the new wood, coloring it to resemble the original piece.

After an area has been cleaned thoroughly with wet steel wool, dry it immediately. Don't allow pools of washing solution to stand on the wood. If your stripper is water-soluble, hosing down the entire piece is not recommended unless special equipment is used. A regular garden hose does not have adequate pressure to really assist in removing the finish, and will wet the wood unnecessarily. High-pressure hoses found in self-service car washes can remove old sludge quickly with a minimum of soaking.

Water-soluble removers should leave the surface perfectly clean, but a final cleanup with turpentine or lacquer thinner is a good precaution. When working with non-water-soluble removers, wipe the wood surface clean with mineral spirits before sanding.

Commercial stripping outlets. If you hate the idea of stripping down furniture, or do not have adequate space to do the job safely, consider taking your work to a professional stripper. The time and energy saved can be directed toward the more creative steps of refinishing.

Commercial stripping outlets have sprung up in every community. There are both franchised and single man operations. They vary greatly in the quality of their work as well as their approach.

Choose a stripping outlet carefully. Furniture can be totally ruined when the wrong stripping methods are used. When choosing an outlet, ask what stripping method is used. Make sure caustic chemicals, blow torches, or other damaging procedures are not used. Lye, even in the hands of an expert, is still risky.

A stripping franchise with a known trade name can be outstanding in one community and less than good elsewhere. If you don't have a friend's recommendation, visit several outlets and judge for yourself. Inquire if the work is guaranteed. A reputable dealer will be pleased to show you samples of his work and explain the process. Care and craftsmanship are important in all phases of furniture refinishing. Stripping is no exception.

Preparing the Surface

Surface repairs. After the furniture has been stripped, wiped clean, and thoroughly dried, it is ready for an initial sanding. At this point, repair all holes, scratches, or tiny dents on the wood's surface.

Plastic wood putty can be used for furniture repair when an opaque finish is planned. Otherwise, use a less obvious filler.

To make a relatively invisible repair, give the furniture an initial sanding and save the dust. Mix the dust with a small amount of aliphatic resin (pale yellow) glue to form a paste. Spread with a spatula or your fingers. Work into damaged area. Apply additional layers of sanding dust until the paste mixture is totally covered. Allow to dry for at least 24 hours, and then smooth the area with gentle sanding.

REMOVING RESIDUAL PAINT PIGMENT AND STAIN

Paint pigments that have impregnated the pores of coarse-grained woods can be virtually impossible to remove.

After all paint and varnish removers have failed, two alternatives remain. One is to sand, seal, and repaint. The second is to integrate the residue of old pigment into the kind of final finish you desire. Make a decision based on what you believe the original finish might have been. Painted furniture usually looks best repainted; however, transparent finishes are not out of the question. The painted pores of old furniture graphically record their wear and age. Such signs of age and character are particularly appropriate for country-style furniture and will be preserved with a transparent finish.

Residual wood stains are less permanent than paint pigment. When they have given the wood an unnatural color (for example, a cherry stain on maple furniture), the entire piece should be bleached.

Other small unidentified stains can be as troublesome as residual stain. Try light sanding first. Water stains that are not deep can be sanded from the surface. When attempting to remove a spot, sand the entire surface evenly. Prolonged sanding in one area will cause more damage than the stain. (See Sanding, page 40.)

If a dark-colored stain remains, the whole piece should be bleached. (Spot bleaching will simply replace the dark stain with a white spot.) It is possible, however, to lighten tiny stains when the bleach is applied sparingly with the fine tip of an artist's brush, then absorbed with a tissue. Apply several times before sanding.

Grease stains on furniture usually come from two sources, animal or vegetable oils. For a stain known to be animal oil, use a spot remover sold for cleaning spots from clothing. Scrub the cleaner into the stained area with a brush. Allow this to dry 24 hours, and repeat the process if the stain persists.

Vegetable oil can sometimes be lifted with acetone, applied as in the earlier spot-bleaching technique for tiny stains. When the origin of the grease stain is unknown, try both methods. It is advisable to use these cleaners outside.

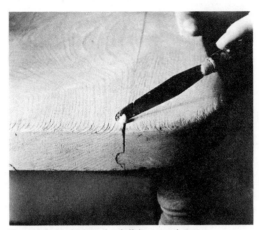

To make almost invisible repairs on bare wood, use a small spatula or palette knife to apply a mixture of sawdust and glue.

BLEACHING

Bleaching will be necessary when all other corrective measures have failed. In the case of old furniture, deep planing and power sanding are not advisable. While they do remove the layers of stain-damaged wood, they also destroy all signs of age.

Bleaching is not without its faults. Bleach, particularly one that needs water rinsing, raises the grain of the wood. In some cases, bleaches deposit a grayish residue that has to be sanded off the wood's surface. And although the wood is lightened, it will not return to its original richness of color and will need to be stained (see page 45) before refinishing.

The material. Wood bleaches are available at most paint specialty stores. If you ask for a wood bleach you will usually receive a two-part bleach. This is a very strong bleach made to remove all color from wood. Two-part bleaches are not recommended for stain removal since they produce a bone-white, lifeless effect.

Gentler bleaches are sold as stain removers. Bottled in plastic, these almost clear solutions contain the bleaching agent sodium hydroxide. They require no mixing and will lighten wood gradually. Their effectiveness is increased by bright sunlight and repeated applications.

A less effective solution of sodium hypochlorite found in household bleaches will also lighten wood to some extent, but requires a final water rinsing.

Oxalic acid, used by professional finishers to lighten wood, is too hazardous for home use.

To begin. Make sure the surface of the wood is clean and smooth. Even coverage is imperative.

Use the same precautions for bleaching that were used for stripping. Cover your skin and eyes, wear old clothing, and work outside.

Read the directions before you start. Pour a small amount of bleach into a plastic container. Use a nylon bristle brush or a sponge to apply bleach evenly to the wood surface. Do not flood bleach or allow it to drip or run.

When you are using a bleaching solution, place furniture in the sun to aid the bleaching action. Wait the prescribed amount of time. Reapply when a lighter color is desired.

Household bleaches will require water rinsing. Other chemical bleaches will indicate how and when they should be neutralized.

After the wood has dried, remove raised grain by light sanding. Water-rinsed furniture should dry 2 to 4 days before final sanding.

SANDING

Sanding is possibly the most neglected area of refinishing. Wood finishers who grudgingly give the wood a fast "once-over" with sandpaper before finishing will frustrate all their efforts to achieve a clear, smooth final finish.

Transparent finishes tend to magnify any imperfections in the wood. Sanding scratches that are not obvious in bare wood will appear un-

---

Tack Rags

Tack rags are excellent for picking up dust and other particles from a wood surface after it has been sanded. This enables the finish to be applied over a clean surface. Tack rags can be bought in many paint stores or can be easily made at home. To make one, fold a large piece of cheesecloth or other coarsely woven cloth into a pad. Wet the pad with water, wring it out, and dampen with turpentine. Now pour a little varnish into the folds. Squeeze and knead the pad until the varnish has penetrated throughout the cloth. Unfold. If there are any dry places, add varnish and knead again. The cloth should be sticky, but not wet enough to drip when squeezed. Sprinkle the cloth with a few drops of water and turpentine before storing and whenever it begins to dry out. Store tack rag in an airtight, rustproof container when it is not in use.

der a clear finish. To avoid this kind of difficulty, several progressive steps in the sanding process are essential.

Sanding should always begin with the smallest grit (finest paper) capable of removing all the wood imperfections. Progress to smaller and smaller grits until you have removed all scratches created by previous sandings. Finally, finish with a very fine grit to achieve a velvet finish.

Power sanding tools have alleviated much of the tedious preparatory sanding, but the final-finish sanding should always be done by hand. Of course, power sanding equipment is not recommended for use on antique furniture or veneer. Aged wood surfaces should be prepared with a gentle hand sanding, using either very fine paper or steel wool.

Tools. Sandpaper of various grades, fine emery cloth, 2/0 steel wool, power sander (optional), lintless cleaning cloths, vacuum cleaner with dusting attachment, small padded sanding block, tack rags (see box on page 40).

Power sanding tools: Some power sanding tools are built for heavy-duty sanding and will remove large amounts of the wood surface very quickly. Obviously, this type of equipment is not suitable for use on furniture. For example, the belt sander is very effective at cleaning up extremely rough surfaces, but if used on furniture could result in disaster. For this reason, furniture finishers need to become aware of the capabilities of various power sanding equipment.

Finishing sanders are easier to control than heavy-duty types. They are available in three styles: the straight-line oscillating sander, the orbital sander, and a combination of both actions in one sander. Since the orbital sander cuts against the grain, it will remove the wood surface more quickly than the straight-line model. However, sanding marks made by the orbital sander will need to be removed with the aid of a straight-line sander. If you can't afford the combination, the straight-line sander is the best compromise.

The material. Purchasing sandpaper for refinishing can be a most confusing experience. Part of the reason lies in the fact that the manufacturers have not been consistent with their product labeling.

Some sandpapers are labeled only according to grade description, such as coarse, medium, fine, and extra fine. Others are labeled according to use: rough sanding, cabinet, finishing, and polishing.

To confuse sandpaper identification even more, two different numbering systems are used to identify the grit size or the grade. The most frequently used system grades papers from 20 (very coarse) through 600 (superfine). An older numbering system is similar to that used for grading steel wool and ranges from 3½ (very coarse) through 0 (medium) to 10/0 (very fine).

Most manufacturers do indicate the type of abrasive material used. When this is not noted on the back of the paper, the color of the grit will help you identify each type. Flint paper is covered with off-white abrasives, garnet is orange, aluminum oxide is tan to gray, and silicon carbide is black.

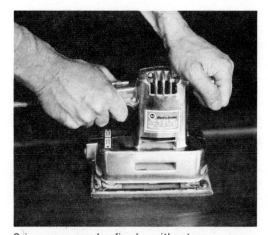

Grip power sander firmly, without applying pressure. Allow the sander to glide evenly over the wood surface.

After you have determined the type and grade of the papers available, you will need more specific information concerning the distribution of abrasive material on the paper's surface. The label "open-coat" indicates that the abrasives cover from 50–70 percent of the backing material and will clog less quickly than those specifying "closed-coat."

The letter designations A, C, D, or E refer to the strength of the paper backing. Coarse papers have more rigid backings, while fine grades need flexibility. The most flexible are designated with an "A."

Emery cloth is another abrasive material that can be useful for smoothing bare wood. Because of its backing, emery cloth can be torn into any shape or size and used with a seesaw motion to smooth hard-to-reach turned and rounded surfaces. Use only fine-grade emery cloth for sanding furniture.

When you are faced with the problem of smoothing intricately carved furniture without removing the detail, use very fine 2/0 steel wool. Steel wool works well on hardwood and can be used to prepare antique wood surfaces without disturbing the wood color. However, steel wool particles have a tendency to become embedded in soft woods and porous hardwoods, making cleanup tedious.

Every sanding application is different and will require its own specific sequence of sandpaper grits, steel wool, and emery cloth. The accompanying sanding chart (page 43) will aid in your selection.

To begin. After the furniture has been stripped, and washed with water or mineral spirits, it is ready for an initial sanding.

Check all surfaces by looking at the wood from various angles in a strong light. Small scratches, dents, and surface blemishes will become evident. Mark these lightly with a pencil so they will remain visible after the wood surface is placed in a horizontal position for sanding.

If the wood surface is very rough to the touch, begin power sanding with a high-medium grit paper such as 80. Normally, a 100 or 120 grit paper will be adequately coarse to remove most imperfections on furniture. This also holds true for hand sanding.

Always sand with the grain! This is especially important when using a straight-line power sander. Also, do not start or turn off a power sander while it is resting on the wood.

As sanding progresses, use finer sandpaper grits. It will not be necessary to use every grit number in a sequence, but it is a good rule never to skip more than one grit size. For example, if you have used 100 grit, it may not be necessary to use 120. Skip 120 grit and progress to 150, 220, 280, as shown in the chart.

Hand sanding is best accomplished with a padded sanding block that protects the wood from sanding scratches. If you purchase a hand sander, make sure it is padded adequately to hold the sandpaper away from the plastic or metal holder. It is simple to construct your own sanding block. Use a small rectangular block of wood and cover one side with felt or sponge for sanding on flat surfaces. Various-shaped blocks can be constructed for specialized applications, such as

PROGRESSIVE STEPS IN SANDING, SMOOTHING, AND POLISHING

	The Process	The Material	Grit Number	Grade Description
1.	Rough sanding on raw wood (power sanding)	Aluminum oxide sandpaper (open-coat)	80–100	Medium to Fine
2.	Initial sanding on semi-smooth raw wood (power or hand sanding)	Aluminum oxide or garnet sandpaper (open-coat) Emery cloth	120, 150 (hardwoods) 220 (softwoods)	Fine Fine Fine
3.	Final smoothing on raw wood (hand sanding)	Garnet sandpaper Steel wool	220, 240, 280	Very Fine Very Fine
4.	Deglossing between coats of finish (hand rubbing)	Steel wool		Extra Fine (3/0–4/0)
5.	Rubbing the final finish (hand rubbing)	Silicon carbide, wet/dry (closed-grain) Steel wool	400	Superfine Extra Fine (4/0)
6.	Final polishing (waxing is optional; power or hand polishing)	Felt or lamb's wool polishing pad		

Abrasives can be identified by grit size and by color (see page 41).

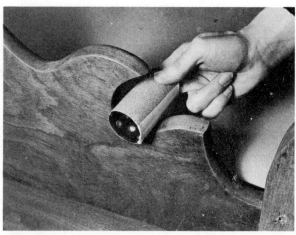

When sanding curved or carved furniture, experiment with different shapes: A hair curler covered with sandpaper fits well into this carved headboard, making it possible to smooth inside surfaces.

a hollow circle for turned legs. Be as ingenious as you can, using any device from a piece of garden hose to a sponge hair curler. Remember, you can also rely on emery cloth and steel wool for those hard-to-reach areas.

Emery cloth can be torn into any shape or size, but always cut sandpaper sheets with scissors to avoid ragged edges. Steel-wool pads are very flexible and will conform to most shapes, but when only a small piece is required, unwind the pad and pull off the amount needed.

Hand sand furniture edges and grain ends with very fine paper. Never use a back-and-forth motion. Exposed pores should be smoothed only in one direction so that they will not absorb large amounts of stain or finish, making them darker than the rest of the wood.

Take care not to lose the original shape of an edge when you are sanding. The exception occurs with new, unfinished furniture. Edges will need to be softened slightly to make the furniture more attractive and to enable it to hold the finish.

In addition, when sanding new wood, it is advisable to wipe wood surfaces with a damp sponge. This will raise the wood "whiskers," allowing for a more uniform smoothing. After sponging, give the surface time to dry. Remove the raised fiber ends with very fine sandpaper.

Sandpaper that becomes clogged will not work well. Use a soft wire brush to remove sanding dust from sandpaper. The vacuum duster attachment can be used to remove sanding dust from furniture.

After each successive sanding step, clean the wood surface with a vacuum or a tack rag.

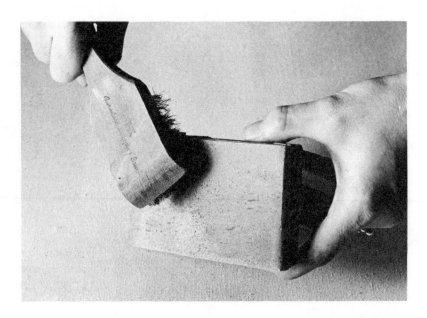

Cleaning sandpaper periodically with a soft wire brush helps to maintain its effectiveness.

STAINING

Improper staining is responsible for a great many failures in furniture finishing. First, discard the idea that staining is a compulsory step in refinishing. We are far beyond the era that decreed all furniture woods should be dark.

Staining, in the contemporary sense, can be a form of shading, as in drawing or painting. When used correctly, stain can bring out certain features of the furniture by heightening the contrast between the darks and lights of the wood.

To stain or not to stain is an aesthetic decision and a matter of personal preference, but it should be pointed out that aged woods usually should not be stained.

When a specific color is required that is different from natural aged wood, it is wiser to start with new, unfinished furniture. The woods in this furniture will have less natural color of their own and will accept stain more readily.

Apart from new woods, staining is a justifiable process when used as a corrective measure on old furniture. For example:

1. Restain to match one piece of a set, such as table and chairs.
2. Restain when bleaching has destroyed the original color.
3. Restain to restore a desirable color that has been faded by wear or the stripping process.
4. Restain a replacement piece to match the original wood finish.

Before deciding on any staining process, consider the coloring effect of the final finish. Even colorless finishes will darken smooth, bare wood. Oil finishes and transparent tung-oil sealer will darken wood slightly more than other transparent finishes. Both have a tendency to deepen the color of the wood figure. To approximate the finished color, moisten your fingertip and rub the wood. Check the color in several areas to become acquainted with the overall range.

Stains can be used to enhance the appearance of new, unfinished furniture when a transparent finish is desired. They can be successfully used for "ageing" copies of traditional furniture. A subtle stain can give new wood the mellowness and warmth that more or less simulates the look of the original furniture.

The material. Before you choose a brand of stain by simply glancing at a color chart, become familiar with the types of stain and their different purposes.

Stains come in four major types: oil stains, water stains, non-grain-raising stains (NGR), and spirit stains. All have advantages and disadvantages, and none is foolproof.

The most commonly available wood stains are the oil stains. These may be pigmented or penetrating. Pigmented oil stains are made by mixing color pigments with a combination of oil and drying agents. These oil stains dry slowly and may be controlled by wiping them off the wood surface, since they do not penetrate deeply. They are relatively opaque, but can usually be thinned with mineral spirits to reduce the intensity of their color.

Pigmented oil stains are best for close-grained woods; they tend to pool in porous woods. Since they can bleed into the finish, they should be fixed with a thinned shellac sealer or a thin coat of the final finish. The drying time for this type of stain cannot be rushed. Read the label before you buy.

Penetrating oil stains are more transparent than pigmented ·types. But as the name implies, they penetrate deeply into the wood and are difficult to remove. Be sure of your color before you start.

Water-based stains will cause the surface of the wood to fuzz or "whisker," which adds steps to the smoothing process. In spite of this fact, water-based stains are favored by furniture manufacturers because they are more transparent, have lasting color quality, and dry quickly. Because they dry quickly, they are best sprayed on. When applying with a brush, acquaint yourself with the drying speed and color by coating test boards of an equivalent wood.

NGR (non-grain-raising) stains are popular because they exhibit most of the desirable properties of water stains without the need for resanding after application. But they, too, are fast-drying and are best applied with professional spray equipment.

Spirit stains are quick-drying, but are not always colorfast. They can bleed into a new finish and must be fixed.

Other, minor types of stains include the pigmented wiping stains. These are particularly suited to accenting knots, scars, and dents in wood when this is desirable. Because the color pigments must be kept in suspension to obtain a uniform coverage, these stains need frequent stirring. They tend to be self-sealing and are available in white (to lighten wood) as well as the usual range of darker colors.

After choosing the type of stain that seems best suited for the job, determine the proper color. Try to visualize the finished piece. Keep the color in mind. Never choose stain by simply asking for the wood color by name. Every brand will have prepared its own version of maple, walnut, and so on. Compare charts and chip samples. When the right shade is not available, mix colors together, always using those of the same type or brand name.

To begin. Each type of stain requires its own technique for application. The manufacturer's instructions should be followed precisely. There are some general principles that will aid in the application of all stains.

First, make sure the surface to be stained is clean and smooth. Superfine sandpaper should be used just before staining—even for new, previously sanded wood. Experiment first. Try the stain on a test board of the same wood, or select an inside section of the furniture for testing. If the stain appears too dark, thin when possible; otherwise allow less penetration time before wiping.

Avoid overloading your brush with stain. Wipe up drips immediately. Do not overlap brush strokes. Brush with the grain of the wood. Stain all inside sections first, leaving the most obvious surfaces until last. Stain the entire piece at one time and make sure all areas are covered.

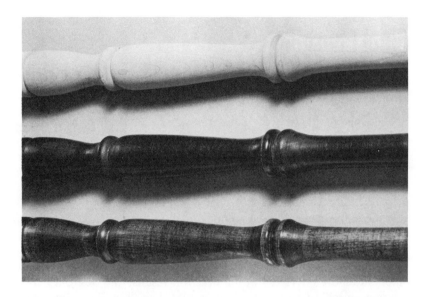

Application of a pigmented wiping stain (top to bottom): Prepared raw wood, ready for staining; after application of a single coat of stain; and after spindle has been wiped to remove excess stain, highlighting the wood.

The darkness and penetration will depend upon the length of time the stain remains on the surface before it is wiped. Wipe the end grains of the wood immediately after stain is applied, since they are more porous and will absorb stain faster than other areas.

The removal of stain by wiping is the creative aspect of staining. Wipe with a plan in mind. Think ahead and wipe stain first from the areas that need to be highlighted. Carved edges, inserts, and so on that must be darkened should be wiped last. Apply even pressure when removing stain with a cloth. Staining streaks destroy the beauty of the wood figure.

Oil stains will take several days to dry, while fast-drying stains will be ready for transparent finishing within 24 hours.

FILLERS

Fillers are used primarily by the manufacturers of new furniture. They are applied over stains or sealer coats (coats of thinned final finish) to fill the coarse grain of woods such as oak, walnut, and mahogany. Fillers are usually colored to match the wood, unless some special effect is desired. Grain that has been filled with a contrasting color is referred to as having a "pickled" finish.

Fillers conceal all pores and make the wood appear perfectly smooth. As the final finish begins to build up on filled wood, the furniture will exhibit a mirrorlike quality which is popular in much of today's furniture.

Few hand finishers strive for these glasslike final finishes. Real enjoyment can be derived from actually feeling the texture of the wood under its finish. For this reason, fillers are not commonly used in refinishing, unless a smooth opaque finish is planned (page 58).

If it is important to restore a contemporary transparent finish to its original smoothness, learn about applying wood fillers from a comprehensive wood-finishing manual or ask your local paint dealer about paste filler products.

Stain can be used to accent carvings and contours, as illustrated in this lamp base made from an old porch post.

Final Finishing

TRANSPARENT FINISHING

With the great variety of quality transparent finishes on the market today, you should have no problem finding a finish that fits your particular needs.

After you have prepared several pieces for refinishing, you may discover that no single transparent finish will satisfy all your requirements. Different finishes are applied for different reasons.

Some refinishers value the original finish to such a degree that they try to preserve the authentic character of the furniture by duplicating the finish as nearly as possible, even without concern for its practicality. Others want a finish that can revitalize old, dry wood. Still others are more interested in the practical results, and desire a long-wearing, durable finish. Some people prefer an "invisible" finish for light, unfinished wood. Whatever the individual considerations, almost everyone is interested in finding a finish that is easy to apply.

Products that advertise a one-step operation, quality results, and easy nonrub application should be viewed with suspicion. Such a product may appear in the future, but it is not yet on the market.

A permanent transparent finish that will preserve wood for another generation's use requires several coats of finishing material, in addition to a generous amount of hand rubbing. Here are some points to keep in mind:

1. Transparent finishing should seal wood against damage from moisture, heat, and wear. And although all transparent finishes do seal the wood, some finishes termed "sealers" penetrate deep into the wood pores. The term "sealer" should not be confused with a sealer coat of finish, which is simply a thinned transparent finish. This thin sealer coat is used to prevent stains from bleeding, and can be the initial coat of finish used on bare wood.

2. More than one coat of transparent finish is required to build a durable base. This means that hand rubbing with very fine sandpaper or steel wool is necessary between coats to remove dust particles or brush marks that might mar the finish. It also deglosses this previous coating, making it possible for the next coat to bond properly. Commercial deglossers, called sanding liquids, were formulated to clean and degloss old finishes (both transparent and opaque) before a new coating is applied. They should not be used between coats of the final finish as a substitute for deglossing by hand sanding or rubbing with steel wool.

After a substantial investment of time and energy goes into preparing a wood surface for finishing, every effort should be made to apply the best and most beautiful finish possible. Before you make a decision based on hearsay or choose a finish because it is available at your corner hardware store, become acquainted with the advantages and disadvantages of each finishing material.

Shellac finishes are often best for small decorative pieces such as this antique lap desk.

Varnish was used to finish the cherry sewing chest pictured here.

The subtle, glowing finish on this golden oak dresser was achieved by using a brushing lacquer to preserve the light color of the unfinished oak.

SHELLAC

Shellac finishes have had a glorious past. Before lacquer came into popularity in the 1920's, shellac was the predominant finish used on all types of furniture.

Shellac enjoys less popularity today because it is much less resistant to water and wear than most of the newer finishes, and it is soluble in alcohol. However, shellac is not without its good points. It is easy to apply when thinned properly, dries quickly, and comes in two different shades—orange and white (clear). White is preferable for refinishing, since orange shellac changes the natural wood color.

Shellac finishes are best for small items that will not receive hard wear or for purely decorative pieces. When thinned, shellac also makes a good sealer coat to protect new woods or to seal stains.

To apply. Shellac should be purchased in small quantities, since it will deteriorate in the can and spoil if stored. When purchasing shellac, you will find it is available in different "cuts." This term refers to the amount of alcohol present in the shellac. A 3-pound cut is the best mixture to buy for finishing furniture. The first two coats will need to be thinned, while the final coats can be applied full strength. When using a 3-pound cut, the thinning ratio for the first coats is 2:5, or 2 parts denatured alcohol to 5 parts shellac. If you still have problems with the application, thin the mixture to a 1:1 ratio.

High humidity can fog a clear shellac, so work in a dry, warm room. Adverse conditions such as a dirty furniture surface or damp weather will prevent shellac from drying properly.

To apply shellac, concentrate your efforts on one section at a time and place the surface to be coated in a horizontal position. Brush on a thinned coating of shellac as quickly and evenly as possible without rebrushing. When thinned to the correct consistency, shellac will flow on smoothly without brush marks.

Rub with 3/0 steel wool and clean with a tack rag (see page 40) after each coat has been allowed to dry completely. Apply three or more coats until the final coat dries to an even gloss. Polish with steel wool, then clean and wax to protect the finish.

LACQUER

The majority of furniture being manufactured today will have a sprayed lacquer finish. Lacquer offers the advantages of a fast-drying finish and with each succeeding coat will build into a deep clear finish capable of magnifying the figure and color of the wood under it. Lacquer wears longer than shellac and is more water resistant. But it will often "check" or crack under extreme changes in temperature.

To take advantage of lacquer's deep-finishing qualities, spray equipment is needed to produce an even build-up of coatings. This may be a problem for the home finisher. Spray cans of high-gloss lacquer just won't do an adequate job. At best, most spray lacquers are tricky and it takes practice to obtain a satisfactory coating. However, spray-can application of semi-gloss lacquer is much easier, and is excellent for fine carvings and small furniture.

Applying brushing lacquer

The best solution for those who do not have spray equipment is to buy lacquer with drying retardants added. This type of lacquer can be applied with a brush. But all brushing lacquers are not equally easy to apply. The most successful and widely used product in this field is not labeled brushing lacquer, but carries only its brand name. It is not a high-gloss finish so is easier to apply and will require less rubbing. Brushing lacquers contain nitrocellulose and a mixture of volatile solvents. Ask your paint dealer for a good brushing lacquer or read the labels.

Before you apply lacquer over an old finish, beware. Lacquer *cannot* be applied over finishing materials that have a mineral spirit base. This includes some stains and wood fillers, as well as most other transparent finishes. Recoat an old transparent finish with lacquer only after you are positive that the original finish was lacquer. (To identify a lacquer finish, see page 10.)

To apply. Work in a clean dust-free area that is both warm and dry. Lacquer and lacquer thinner are flammable mixtures and should not be used near an open flame.

If you are applying lacquer to bare wood, thin the first coat to seal the wood. Add lacquer thinner until you obtain a watery brushing liquid. Apply this first coat generously and let it soak into the wood. After this has dried, rub with 3/0 steel wool and clean away all filings. Next, apply a full-strength coat of lacquer, this time taking care to avoid brush marks. Use a good bristle brush and flow on with even strokes, tipping up the brush at all edges to avoid runs.

Allow this coating to dry 2 hours, or longer in humid weather. Wipe with 3/0 steel wool, clean, and recoat. After a 24-hour drying period the finish can be rubbed to produce the desired sheen.

VARNISH

Varnish has in the past been a standard with wood finishers. Available in gloss, semi-gloss, and satin, it is more resistant to stain and wear than shellac. But ordinary varnish has disadvantages. It is not easy to apply. Furthermore, it dries slowly and tends to pick up dirt particles from the air. The particles may be removed with difficulty while the finish is wet or they can be rubbed out after the finish is totally dry. The problem remains that it is an impossible task to protect a newly finished piece from all dust and dirt for 12 to 36 hours while the varnish dries. Even after the varnish appears dry, a wait of three to five days is required before the finish can be safely rubbed with 3/0 steel wool.

When applied and dried properly, varnish can produce a handsome hard finish. But after all the work and worry, a regular oil varnish will never be as resilient and durable as the new polyurethane varnish products.

Regular oil varnishes are useful for recoating old varnished finishes that need revitalizing, or for similar jobs that do not require numerous coatings. However, except in these few cases, regular varnish is better replaced by one of the long-wearing urethane finishes or an easy-to-apply tung-oil transparent sealer.

POLYURETHANE VARNISH

The urethane-type synthetic varnishes have revolutionized the paint and varnish industry. Polyurethane, as well as other quality urethane finishes, can withstand the tortures of water, chemicals, grease, and weather without cracking, peeling, or staining. These varnishes are not only excellent for spraying, but can also be brushed onto bare wood.

Polyurethane varnishes cannot be applied over old shellac or lacquer finishes. They should be used over specially formulated stains and fillers. Read labels to discover products compatible with urethanes. They also can be applied over most regular varnishes that have been deglossed.

Polyurethane varnishes are nonpenetrating. They fortify the surface of the wood with a hard protective coating. They are a fine choice for finishing new wood, or wood that has not been dried by harsh chemical stripping and age. Synthetic varnishes are recommended for use on table tops and counters that are subject to a great deal of wear, water, and abuse.

To apply. The wood surface must be free from dirt, wax, and finish removers. Before you begin, you will need to plan a finishing schedule. Do not allow more than 48 hours drying time between coats of urethane. After the finish is allowed to cure two to four days, it will harden completely, making it impossible for additional coats to adhere properly. A suggested finishing schedule might be one coating each day over a three-day period.

When brushing on urethane finishes, thin the first coat according to the manufacturer's suggestion. The thinned coat can then be brushed or wiped into the bare wood to seal the pores. Although this finish is fast-drying to the touch, allow it to dry overnight to insure a hard finish for rubbing. The second and third coats should be applied full strength with a brush in a manner similar to brushing lacquers. Use 3/0 steel wool, or superfine sandpaper if you prefer, for deglossing between coats. Clean the surface completely after each rubbing. The final finish can be polished with superfine sandpaper until the desired amount of gloss has been removed.

TRANSPARENT TUNG-OIL WOOD SEALER AND FINISH

Unlike the finishes reviewed previously, transparent tung oil does not stay on the surface of the wood, but penetrates deep into the wood pores. This type of finish can revive old, dried wood and prevent further damage. It builds up a gloss finish that resembles varnish, while it becomes an integral part of the wood. It strengthens as it seals.

Perhaps the most important plus for the home wood finisher is that transparent tung oil is simple to apply. It eliminates the problems of brush marks and sags. When completely dry, it will not become brittle, shrink, or "check" when exposed to temperature changes. As the finish penetrates, it gives the wood a new resilience, allowing for equal amounts of expansion, contraction, and moisture-level changes throughout the wood.

Applying tung oil

Examples of two different approaches to furniture finishing. The handcrafted walnut cradle on the right was painstakingly hand rubbed with an oil finish to preserve its natural beauty. The walnut Victorian dresser below was finished with a hard polyurethane varnish for durability.

A tung-oil finish is resistant to alcohol, grease stains, and even hot water. If a portion of the finish becomes worn, it can be deglossed and recoated without being removed. Dirt and grime can be washed off with mild soap and water. Waxing is not necessary.

Transparent tung oil is compatible with most fillers and wood stains. It can be applied over old shellac or varnish. However, to obtain the full benefit of penetration, old finishes should be removed.

Tung oil is a natural oil derived from the nuts of the tung-oil tree. When processed into the finishing product, this honey-colored oil will deepen the natural color of wood, making most staining unnecessary.

Tung oil contains its own natural drying agent; it must be fresh to dry properly. Buy as needed, and reseal the container after each use.

Penetrating sealers include not only tung oil, but a variety of synthetic resin sealers. All preserve wood from insect attack, warping, and water damage, making them highly desirable finishes for all wood products. The synthetic resin sealers are capable of transforming the outer layers of wood fiber into a plastic-like material. This characteristic is desirable in some cases, but transparent tung-oil sealers are better suited to retaining the natural beauty of furniture woods.

One word of caution! Transparent tung oil is relatively slow-drying compared to lacquer and polyurethane finishes. Allow the recommended drying time so that the finish can cure properly.

To apply. Read directions and suggestions on the label. Work in a warm but well-ventilated room. Pour a small amount of tung oil into a wide-mouthed container. Cover the floor or table under your work. Dip both hands into the oil and rub onto the furniture, continuing this process until the entire piece is covered. Don't forget the underside or bottom. All surfaces must be covered to insure equal strength and prevent warping.

The first coat may be absorbed quickly, depending on the heat of your hands and the dryness of the wood. Wipe off any excess with a clean cloth.

The second coat can be applied almost immediately if the wood is very dry or has been commercially stripped of its finish. The number of coats will depend upon the age and condition of the raw wood.

Let the second coat dry thoroughly, at least 36 hours, or longer in humid climates. Sealers can be deceptive. Although they may feel dry to the touch, they might still be damp deep in the pores of the wood. Patience is the best policy when waiting for a finish to dry.

When you are ready for the next coat, inspect the piece for uneven covering or dry spots. Concentrate your efforts on these "thirsty" areas first, giving them a generous rubbing of tung oil. Continue to other areas. Use your fingertips to smooth out all excess oil. Let dry. Inspect your finish again, this time for luster as well as even coating.

Degloss the dry finish with 3/0 steel wool. The furniture is now ready for another coating. Dried, parched wood will absorb as many as five coats, while relatively new wood can be adequately finished with three coats. Continue to recoat, dry, and degloss until the finish appears uniform, without dull spots.

The wood by now has built up a fine glossy sheen, which you may wish to preserve. If this is the case, the application of the final coat is best laid on flat surfaces, such as table tops, with a very soft brush or cloth. Using great care, dip the brush or cloth into the tung oil and pull it evenly across the surface of the wood, making sure that no areas are left uncovered and that there is no overlapping of the finish. For more ornamental furniture, your hands continue to be the best tools for applying oil.

To obtain a deep-stain sheen, let this final coat dry a week or more. When you are sure the finish is firm, remove as much of the shine as you desire with 3/0 or 4/0 steel wool. Dust with a soft cloth to remove any particles of steel wool, then rub with your hands.

Waxing is not necessary with a transparent tung oil and could be harmful if you have not allowed the finish to "cure" for several months.

OIL FINISHES

Oil finishes continue to be used by those who enjoy hand-rubbed wood. When a piece of wood is pleasurable to handle, hand rubbing can become a labor of love that continues almost indefinitely.

From the standpoint of the purist, the oil from human hands remains the best finishing oil. But formulas, materials, and processes for hand rubbing are varied. Each hand finisher, because of his individual experience with wood, will recommend his favorite concoction. The most commonly used formula combines boiled linseed oil and turpentine. The ratio of linseed oil to turpentine may vary from a 3:1 to a 1:1 mixture. In another formula, equal parts of white vinegar are combined with the boiled linseed oil and turpentine. A rubbing combination favored by antique finishers contains refined beeswax dissolved into equal parts of boiled linseed oil; this is applied to the wood while still warm.

Yet another formula for a rubbed-oil finish combines the ingredients of the famed French polishing: shellac, denatured alcohol, and boiled linseed oil in equal parts.

Whatever oil finish you prefer, make sure that you purchase only *boiled* linseed oil for hand rubbing. Raw linseed oil should not be used for furniture finishing.

It is also possible to purchase prepared oil finishes. These products claim to enable you to obtain the authentic hand-rubbed quality with less actual rubbing. As always, the final finish will depend upon careful application. The biggest advantage of prepared oil finishes is that they dry quickly and are less sticky. Like all oil finishes, they require periodic recoating to maintain the finish.

To apply. Apply only to clean, prepared wood. Saturate a rag in the oil mixture and rub thoroughly into one small area at a time until the entire piece is uniformly coated. A warm mixture will provide more penetration. It also tends to darken the wood. But be warned: Do not heat an oil mixture directly! Use a double boiler or other method to keep the flammable mixture away from the heat source.

Rubbing oil into wood to create a soft finish

When the wood refuses to absorb more oil, wipe off the excess with a soft, clean cloth. Otherwise, the excess oil will form a sticky residue. If this occurs, use paint remover to spot-clean the oil build-up.

Now, rub the surface briskly to polish the oil into the wood. Use a hard, tightly woven cloth such as denim. Wait two or three days and apply another oil coating in the same manner.

After this initial base finish has been established, wait two weeks to a month before applying additional coats. The number of coats will depend upon the wood and its ability to absorb the finish. After the desired luster has been created, maintain this finish by reoiling and polishing once or twice a year.

WAX FINISHES

Although waxing and polishing are usually done to maintain and preserve transparent finishes, it is possible to use wax as the primary finishing agent.

Paste wax finishes are favored for their beautiful soft luster and for their mellowing effect on furniture woods. Waxing is a nearly foolproof method of finishing, although it will be less permanent and wear-resistant than harder finishes.

The cardinal rule for finishing with paste wax is: *Never apply wax to bare wood.* Paste wax is impossible to remove from the pores of wood and may spoil the appearance of the furniture as it discolors with age. Avoid this problem by sealing bare wood with white shellac before applying wax. After the wood is sealed, wax can be applied and removed without damaging the furniture.

The tan-colored paste wax available at all grocery stores is an acceptable finishing wax. But if you are willing to search them out, the carnauba-type waxes (from the Brazilian wax palm) are harder and will produce a long-wearing, high-luster finish.

Wax products that contain imported carnauba wax (usually about 50 percent) are found in paint and hardware stores. They are available in colors ranging from clear to brown. Choose a clear wax for light fine-grained woods. Dark porous woods will require a darker color that will not be visible after the wax builds up on the surface of the wood.

To apply. Clean and smooth the wood surfaces as described in the preceding chapter. Dilute white shellac with denatured alcohol. Brush on evenly and let dry. A second coat of shellac sealer may be advisable for coarse-grained woods.

After the sealer coat is dry, remove any shellac build-up with 3/0 steel wool. Clean the wood surface. You are now ready to wax.

Apply the first coat with a clean steel-wool pad (1/0 or 2/0), or a soft cloth. This coat must be thin. Don't overload, but apply evenly, working with the grain. Allow this coat to dry 5 to 15 minutes according to the manufacturer's instructions. Begin the polishing by first removing any excess wax with a soft cloth. Then buff the furniture, preferably with an electric polisher, such as the polishing attachment available with most sanders.

Repeat this process and polish after each application. Two thin applications of carnauba wax may be sufficient. After the proper wax base has been established, rewax only when the finish needs renewing. A heavy wax build-up will not enhance the wood.

NUDE WOOD FINISHES

The present concern over the scarcity of quality furniture woods is reflected in our growing appreciation for all types of wood. This is evidenced in contemporary furniture. The "no-finish" finish or "nude" finish allows furniture woods such as birch, ash, maple, oak, and even pine to remain light and natural.

The illusion of no-finishing is produced in several ways. The goal is to transform raw wood into serviceable furniture without hiding the wood's natural beauty. This can be accomplished by using penetrating sealers of synthetic resin or urethane on soft woods such as pine. These sealers penetrate deeply, hardening the wood until its durability equals that of hardwood.

When working with uneven grain or knotty pine, use a *very* thin wiping coat of zinc white paint or white stain to even the wood figure. After the paint or stain has been wiped thoroughly and has dried, use a urethane or other transparent finish compatible with the undercoating.

Butcher-block furniture is finished by the oil rubbing method (see page 56). A clear vegetable oil is a good choice for tables or other food-oriented furniture. Otherwise, boiled linseed oil can be used.

Generally, light-colored hardwoods can be finished with water-clear varnish or semi-gloss brushing lacquer. All nude wood finishes must be dulled to emphasize the wood, not the finish.

Clear carnauba-type wax will also provide a nude finish on hardwoods (see preceding section). Remember to wax only after the wood has been sealed.

OPAQUE FINISHING

Opaque finishing has played a major role in the history of American furniture. Our ancestors were extremely innovative in the art of furniture painting and decorating. Decorated furniture has left a record of personal expression, as well as capturing the essence of the American creative spirit. Immigrants were able to translate traditional symbols into new forms of expression. To them, opaque finishing was not only a way to protect wood surfaces from hard wear or to emulate precious woods; it was, more importantly, a cultural link to their past. Rather than being an art limited to furniture designers, opaque finishing developed in various parts of the country as a true folk expression.

We have learned to value the painted furniture of the past. Unfortunately, furniture decorating is no longer continued in the same creative tradition. Nowadays most of our decorated furniture begins as a prepared kit. The care and craftsmanship necessary to produce a beautiful transparent finish are often forgotten when paint is applied. We have come to value the opaque finish less because we have failed to recognize the positive factors of interest and balance that painted

Facing page: A tung-oil finish revitalized the worn and water-damaged wood of this handsome old icebox.

A "nude" finish was the ideal choice for this pine table built to display samples of embroidery from Bedouin wedding dresses. (From the collection of Gail Steinberg.)

A wax finish enhances the soft, mellow quality of the wood in this oak dining table and chairs.

furniture supplies to our living environment. Painted furniture is not only practical and durable, but is also one of the most creative forms of finishing. The color and design possibilities are limitless.

The material. The first step in obtaining a beautiful opaque finish is to choose the correct materials. Select only quality enamels when you are ready to paint furniture. Even the least expensive fir or pine furniture deserves the best possible finish. The time and effort spent in finishing will be repaid if the final finish is durable, colorfast, and washable.

Water-soluble latex paints usually will not provide an adequate finish for furniture unless they are coated with a hard transparent finish. Oil base enamels are most commonly used for furniture; however, colored lacquers are very successful when spray equipment is available. Spray-can enamels and lacquers are preferable for special jobs such as wicker, wrought iron, or intricately carved furniture.

Enamels are available in high-gloss, semi-gloss, and satin finishes. As with varnish, the high-gloss enamel finish can be expected to wear best, and is the most desirable for a hand-rubbed finish. But a semi-gloss enamel is an acceptable compromise if hand rubbing is considered too time consuming.

Remember that enamels will not produce a hard finish with the application of one coat after another. Unlike transparent finishes, enamel finishes require a base formed by special primers or under-coatings. Most paint manufacturers offer compatible undercoatings for their enamels. If there is no such undercoating for the enamel you choose, ask the paint dealer to recommend one. When deep, rich colors are planned, the undercoating should be tinted. Never apply enamel to bare wood!

A sealer coat is mandatory for new, untreated wood. A coat of thinned shellac will seal knots and prevent sap from seeping through an enameled surface. However, to assure an even opaque finish when enameling over wild-grained plywood, use a synthetic resin sealer (see page 55) before the primer coat.

Color. The color range of enamels is fantastic. You no longer have to depend on the hand-mix methods, or the uncertainty of mixing your own colors from paint pigment tubes. Find a paint store with a color-mixing machine and choose from over a thousand color possibilities or any shade in between. The color formula will be recorded. This will enable you to purchase additional enamel in the identical color at a later date.

Don't play it safe by buying standardized colors off the shelf until you have investigated all the color possibilities. The excitement of discovering a vibrant color can spark your imagination. Also, familiarize yourself with special opaque finishes. Here your choice will range from bright colors of the contemporary wet-look to the mellow tones of enamels compounded to simulate the old milk paint finishes.

If you are not experienced with enamel colors, it may be difficult to visualize an entire painted piece from a test chip of color. There is no sure way to judge the final intensity of the dried color. The safest method is to test the color by applying the undercoating, then painting a part that doesn't show, such as the bottom of a table or the back of a chest. If the dried color is not what you expected, return the enamel to the store for additional mixing. (This is not always possible with off-the-shelf premixed paints.)

To apply. Smooth all surfaces of new or stripped wood as carefully as if you were preparing for a transparent finish. Make repairs, such as gluing, but do not patch the surface at this time. When working with new furniture, remove any excess dried glue from joints.

New soft woods such as pine will require a shellac sealer coat to prevent the sap from discoloring the enamel. Old furniture will also need to be sealed when traces of the original stain remain. Apply an initial sealer coat of half shellac and half denatured alcohol over all knots or discolored grain. After this is dry, scuff lightly with steel wool and apply a thinned coat of shellac to the entire piece. (Or a coat of synthetic resin sealer can be used over uneven-grained plywood.) When the sealer coat has dried, scuff with steel wool and wipe clean. The surface is now ready for patching.

Patch wooden furniture with an oil base compound such as wood putty or plastic wood. Surface patching is particularly important for old furniture that has been badly damaged, making transparent finishing no longer feasible. Deep holes and pits should be overfilled, since patching compounds shrink as they dry. Any excess can be removed with sandpaper after the repair is dry. Use the glue/sanding dust combination (see page 39) for nail holes and small patching problems. Overfill holes, dry, sand, and clean.

Paste wood fillers are rarely used, since the valuable coarse-grained woods such as walnut, which require such fillers, are not usually painted. A full-bodied undercoating will normally smooth the surface of most woods. When a satin rubbed finish is desired on open-grained oak, however, it may be wise to use a filler before the undercoating.

Wood fillers are easy to apply and need not be colored for opaque finishing. Follow the directions on the label for using them. Wipe off all excess filler within the prescribed amount of time, using a coarse cloth to rub across the grain.

Be as careful when applying the first undercoating as you would with the final enamel. Any runs or drips left on the surface will remain evident.

Do not dip the brush directly into the can of undercoating or enamel. Pour out the desired amount into a wide-mouthed container or paint bucket. Close the original can tightly to prevent scum from forming on the surface of the paint. Hardened paint particles must not be mixed into the paint. Where a film of hard paint exists, remove carefully before the paint or enamel is stirred.

Never overfill the brush. Begin brushing in one direction. Later, smooth out the fresh layer of paint with the tip of the brush.

To produce an extremely hard, smooth finish on bare or sealed wood, use two coats of undercoating plus two coats of enamel. Sand and clean between each coating. This method is desirable, but not

Facing page: Before repainting, several layers of old paint were removed from this iron bed. Two coats of rust-proof spray provided the undercoating. Finally, several thin coats of spray enamel were used to build up a smooth, lustrous finish.

This example of two-color antiquing began as an unfinished pine reproduction. After applying an undercoating, the exterior was painted blue, the interior "gun metal." The front panel was covered with a decoupage print. Later, antiquing glazes were applied to each color and to the decoupage. The entire piece was sealed with a compatible transparent sealer.

mandatory, if you intend to change enamel color frequently. A shortened procedure will not greatly sacrifice the finished quality and will allow for later recoating.

For a shortened process, after the first undercoating has dried, smooth it with very fine sandpaper, using a sanding block. Make the next coat a mixture of half enamel and half undercoating (they should be the same brand). Let dry, then sand and clean before applying the final coating of enamel. Use the recommended thinner if enamel is stiff and pulls against the brush.

Furniture that needs a single recoating of enamel to update the color or revive a faded color must be totally cleaned and sanded, or deglossed using a liquid sanding product. When the old enamel finish is worn, marked, or scarred, sand the area lightly and retouch with an application of undercoating. Continue to recoat and smooth until the damaged areas are level with the rest of the surface. Finally, apply a single coat of enamel. Two coats may be necessary when covering a contrasting color. In this case, thin the first coat, allow to dry, sand, and apply the final coat full strength.

An enamel finish, like transparent finishes, must be allowed to cure before the final rubbing is attempted. The amount of drying time will depend upon the weather and the type of enamel used. Read the label. The proper drying time will be listed, and in some instances the curing time as well. Proper curing will probably take up to two weeks.

Enamel finishes benefit from hand rubbing in the same way as transparent finishes. Rubbing removes any traces of brush marks, dust, or bubbles, making the surface perfectly smooth as it mellows the gloss into a soft glow. Pumice and oil or pumice and water are used for rubbing enameled finishes. Combine FFF pumice, or finer, with water or light oil to form a paste. Rub this mixture onto the surface with a thick felt pad. A child's blackboard eraser is a handy rubbing tool, but it must be new and free from dust. Rub only in the direction of the grain, even over opaque finishes. Work in a well-lighted area and check the surface often to assure an even smoothing. After the desired amount of gloss has been removed, clean the surface with a dry cloth. Wax can be applied to an enameled finish, but this remains a matter of preference.

Special opaque finishes. Antiquing and frostiquing are two popular opaque-finishing techniques that require the use of a glaze over the original enamel color. Antiquing glazes are dark and tend to age the furniture, while light frostique glazes soften pastel shades. Although the kit that supplies both the enamel and the glaze is readily found, large paint and hardware stores now stock enamels and glazes separately. An open stock of these products will allow you to create your own color combinations, and permit you to buy the appropriate amount of each type of material.

When executed properly, antiquing and frostiquing are not shortcut methods. You will need to follow the exact procedure recommended for opaque finishing before the glaze is applied. In addition, the final coat of enamel must be "roughed" with 3/0 steel wool to provide a dull base for the glaze. After the glaze has been applied, wiped, and dried, a hard transparent finish will be required to seal the glaze color when latex enamels are used. Read the labels to find a compatible transparent finish.

The glazed finish can be used for shading and is most effective when applied to carved or distressed (age-marked) furniture. Shading is accomplished by wiping the glaze color off while it remains wet. The procedure for removing a glaze by wiping parallels that for shading with stain (page 45). Places to be highlighted will be wiped first, leaving small amounts of the glaze material clinging to rough edges and deposited in corners.

Graining, veining, and other texturing of opaque finishes can also be created with the use of a glaze. Rarely are these effects done convincingly. If you have ever admired the flamboyant approach to furniture graining produced by Early American craftsmen, you will come to realize that deception was not the primary goal. We, too, should approach glazing from the standpoint of decoration. (See the section Decorative Texturing on page 72.)

At the other end of the spectrum, the wet-look enamels were designed to change dull, lifeless pieces into contemporary furniture, or to brighten a room with an eclectic decor. These enamels are available in different styles, but most are water-base latex. The two-step process, using latex enamel followed by a gloss coat of a compatible transparent finish, will provide a more permanent finish than the use of latex alone. Whichever method you choose, do not apply latex paint to bare-wood furniture. Seal or prime the wood to avoid any grain-raising effects caused by water-base paints.

To create interesting contrasts, different opaque finishes can be used in one room setting. Compare the wet look of the green campaign furniture pictured here with the antiqued finish of the bookcase and the satin finish on the bentwood chair.

Creative Furniture Techniques

People have highly individual requirements for the furniture they wish to have in their homes. Mass-produced furniture obviously cannot fulfill all of these requirements. Nor do many people have the time, interest, and ability to design and build furniture to meet their needs. Fortunately, it is not necessary to choose between these extremes. You can strike a happy compromise by creatively adapting furniture to your own needs and desires.

Gathering together various ideas and different people into one living environment brings limitless possibilities. Let your knowledge and experience in other creative areas flow into innovative ideas for furniture and room design. Your home can become a visually pleasing oasis reflecting the personalities and the interests of its creators.

Following are some suggestions and techniques that may assist you in creating with furniture.

DECOUPAGE

The early engravings executed by eighteenth-century European artisans first inspired the art of decoupage. These elegant prints were colored, cut out, and preserved under many coats of finish. And it was a natural progression for this technique of decoupage to be applied to furniture. Craftsmen skilled in decoupage simulated the extravagant hand-painted furniture then so popular with French and Italian nobility.

Today, reproductions of eighteenth-century engravings are available for those who enjoy re-creating the art in its original form. These engravings and similar antique-print reproductions continue to be the major source of decoupage design. But there is also a wealth of contemporary printed matter from which to choose. It is not necessary to rely on craft shop designs for your inspiration. Instead, transform the medium into a very personal form of expression, creating with pictures from current magazines, posters, cartoons, or your own drawings and designs.

Tools. Scissors, sealer, printed designs or photos, water-soluble glue, clean cloth, brayer or other small roller, tack rag (page 40), #400 wet/dry sandpaper, 4/0 steel wool, decoupage varnish or other finish, clean brush.

To begin. Decoupage can be applied over varnished or enameled surfaces that are in good repair. A varnish finish must be cleaned and deglossed with sanding liquid or sanded. An opaque painted surface should be sanded lightly and washed with mineral spirits to clean. Some opaque finishes will need to be sealed before decoupage varnish is applied; test the paint for "bleeding" before you begin by applying the varnish to an inconspicuous place.

Raw or bare wood must be sealed before the decoupage print is applied. If you want to retain the natural color of the wood, use

Facing page: "George Washington Dresser" by Michael Jones and Michael Fajans. To create this larger-than-life portrait, the artists projected the image, taken from an engraving, and painted it directly on the furniture. The background is white enamel. The portrait is done in acrylics. Finally, the entire piece was "aged" and sealed with coats of white and orange shellac.

thinned shellac or decoupage sealer. If you prefer to darken it, use pigmented sealer or non-bleeding stain. While the sealer is drying, prepare the print or picture for your decoupage design.

The first step in preparing the picture is to seal it. Do this before you cut it. Brush on a coating of diluted white glue or a special decoupage print sealer. When using a magazine photograph, seal both sides to prevent the printed material on the reverse side from showing through the front of the picture.

Cutting a print for decoupage takes practice. Curved-bladed decoupage scissors are preferable. Whatever type of scissors you use, keep in mind that the outline of the print should have irregular edges. Hold the scissors with one hand, and feed the printed material into the blades with the other. Wiggle the paper back and forth to avoid a straight cut. If your design consists of several separate pieces, assemble these and consider your final design before you apply glue.

Apply a thin, smooth film of water-soluble glue to the wood surface with your fingers. Place the print over the glue and press. Wipe off any excess glue, then roll the print with a brayer to smooth it completely. Wipe off glue around the print. Do not overlap designs. This will cause lumps in your final finish.

After the glue is dry, you are ready for the first coat of decoupage finish. Varnish, lacquer, or decoupage varnish can be used. Follow the directions on the container for drying and deglossing. Usually it will take ten coats of the finish to build a surface that can be sanded without damage. Even then, great care must be taken when sanding over the print. Use #400 wet/dry (waterproof) sandpaper. Keep the surface and the sandpaper moist at all times. A small amount of detergent added to the water will prevent scratching. 4/0 steel wool can be used for hard-to-reach areas. Clean with a tack rag.

Apply approximately ten more coats and wet-sand again. Most pieces of furniture will require thirty or more coats to submerge the print adequately into the finishing material.

To eliminate some of the final hand rubbing, use a low-luster varnish for the last two coats. Smooth the final finish with 4/0 steel wool, wax, and buff.

(Top left) Broken and marred furniture like this old sewing kit table doesn't have to be thrown away, but can be given a new lease on life with the use of decoupage. (Bottom left) After total finish removal, sanding, and simple repair, a new coat of paint was used as the background for Victorian-style decoupage prints. The sewing table was then finished with numerous coats of transparent decoupage finish and hand rubbed.

This supergraphic design was created with the mask-and-spray technique (see page 72).

Decorative painting and texturing can give new life to ordinary furniture. The textured finish on the bench below was created by using a glaze of thinned brown paint over white enamel. Sawtooth pieces of cardboard were used to produce the pattern. The design on the "Greyhound Chair" by Dean Pingrey (right) was executed in a combination of acrylic paint and silver enamel, and then sealed. The cedar chest combines texturing and painting over a white enamel background. The design, in ordinary poster paint, was sealed with a glossy coat of transparent finish.

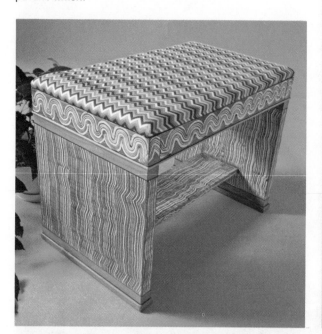

Note: *The following creative techniques are to be used on an opaque finish that is completely dry. After the decoration or design is applied, a final coat of transparent finish will be required to seal the design. Water-base enamels or acrylic paints are recommended as an opaque finish for decorative techniques unless otherwise stated.*

STENCILING

Tools. Oil stencil board, mat knife, masking tape, spray ink or regular stencil ink, and various-sized round stencil brushes.

Technique. The bronze stenciling with its subtle shading and three-dimensional qualities so popular in America during the mid-nineteenth century has fallen into disuse. And although the techniques for applying metallic particles to nearly dry varnish are known, they are used primarily for the restoration of earlier works. This need not imply that stenciling is no longer a valid method of decorating furniture. With the current availability of spray-can inks, creamy metallic pastes, and specialized stencil papers, the art of stenciling has yet to reach its full potential. The techniques are simplified; designing for the medium takes thought and preparation.

The ancient art of stencil design relied heavily on intricate patterns cut from folded paper. The detail of the design related to the number of folds and the dexterity of the designer. These paper patterns were unfolded and used directly for stenciling. Today an additional step is recommended: transfering the pattern to oil stencil board, a specially prepared stencil board that has an oily finish. Apply your paper pattern to the stencil board with a thin coating of rubber cement. Cut out the design, using a very sharp mat knife. Peel off the paper pattern and clean the glue from the board before printing.

When designing a stencil, keep in mind that the sections cut away will become the printed area. This also applies to silk-screen printing, which is feasible for furniture when the printing surface is perfectly flat. Since that is rarely the case, stenciling remains a more useable printing technique.

If a multi-colored, overlapping design is planned, a stencil will be needed for each color. The separate stencils must register correctly to form the final design. Peepholes cut in the outer edges of the stencil board should help to solve the registration problem.

Several colors can also be brushed on over a single stencil when the design does not merge, bridge, or overlap. Use a separate stencil brush for each color and apply all the colors before the stencil is removed. When different colors are in close proximity, allow each color to dry thoroughly before proceeding.

Make sure the stencil is taped firmly to the furniture before you begin printing. Stencil spray, ink, and paste all require different methods of application. Read the instructions on the container or ask about stenciling techniques at the art supply store where you buy stenciling supplies.

Many of th early stencils were outlined in a contrasting or a darker color to accentuate the design. If this effect is desired, outline with a fine felt-tip pen that contains waterproof ink. Finally, cover the entire surface of the furniture with a coating of transparent finish to seal and preserve your work.

Before you begin, test the transparent finish to make sure it will not cause the stencil colors to "bleed." Spray application is best. If you are not experienced in the use of spray cans, spray only a thin coating of semi-gloss lacquer or synthetic varnish to seal the stencil design. After this is dry, recoat the entire piece using a brush and the *same* transparent finish in liquid form.

STRIPING AND SUPERGRAPHIC DESIGNS

Stripes were originally painted freehand. The artist dipped a needle-like brush into a mixture of paint pigment and varnish and then applied the mixture directly to the furniture.

Striping is still an attractive means of emphasizing design areas, colors, and carvings on furniture. But today new, simpler methods make it possible for an amateur to draw a very professional-looking stripe.

All you need is a ruler, masking tape, two or three coins, and several felt-tip pens in different waterproof colors. Choose the point size of the pens to correspond to the width of stripe you desire. Tape coins to the underneath side of a ruler or other straightedge to avoid smearing the line. The ruler can then be secured to the furniture with tape to hold it steady while you draw.

It is wise to practice drawing stripes on paper first. For problem areas, such as striping around the spindle of a chair, mask off the stripe with tape. This is also a good technique to use for metallic striping. Gold or other metallic paints can be sprayed after complete masking. Cream or paste metallic paints are applied directly with the fingers. Seal with a transparent finish after the stripe is totally dry.

Masking tape is handy for blocking off large stripes or producing supergraphic designs that can be spray-painted. Form a sharp-edged design, using the lines of the tape, or cut extra-wide tape to produce gentle curves that can follow the lines of the furniture.

When large areas of color are to be added on top of an enamel finish, degloss the initial coating by sanding or use a flat finish for it. Later, the entire piece can be sealed with a transparent finish that is compatible with the colored enamels or acrylic paint used for the design.

DECORATIVE TEXTURING

Texturing an opaque finish with a contrasting color is a form of decoration often found in Early American furniture painting.

All texturing techniques should begin with experimentation. Here, a water-soluble paint is a must. If your first design fails to meet your expectation, simply remove it with a damp cloth before the paint is dry. Fast-drying, latex-type paints are not only removable, but also make it possible to use different colors in rapid succession, allowing for spontaneity in the creation of a design.

An example of painted pine furniture, c. 1830, this tall chest of drawers is decorated with painted flowers and thumbprints. (From the Collections of Greenfield Village and the Henry Ford Museum.)

When you wish to create an overall textured pattern, try a dry sponge or an old scruffy brush dipped in paint. Dab the paint on the surface or apply the color in one direction, using even strokes. The paint for texturing will need to be thinned to a glaze consistency that will allow the base color to show through.

For an even livelier pattern, draw designs in the textured glaze with a combing tool made from the corrugated portion of corrugated cardboard or from ordinary cardboard with "teeth" cut in it. Other materials such as crumpled plastic, wadded cellophane, or pieces of styrofoam are good tools for drawing swirls and creating patterns in the glaze color. Continue to experiment until you discover a texture that makes your design unique.

PHOTOGRAPHIC TECHNIQUES

Photographic techniques for furniture? There is now a photosensitive material that can be sprayed on almost any surface, including finished or smooth wood. You then print pictures on this surface in a darkroom. Consider this method for creating a photo collage. The clean designs of the furniture cube or the Parson's table lend themselves well to such photographic treatment.

When you do not have a darkroom available, re-create a photographic image by painting directly on the furniture. Use a slide projector and a regular photographic slide or one that you have specially prepared. Project this image directly onto the furniture. Outline the details, making notes of the colors, or reduce all color to dark and light tones for a special effect. Fill in the design in a free fashion, or create a more faithful reproduction by reprojecting the image and revising your design as you progress.

FURNITURE AS ART

It goes without saying that all forms of painting and drawing are usually applicable to furniture. For instance, if you consider the mural a relevant form of art, why not design a mini-mural to transform a faded cupboard or chest of drawers? Or begin your experimentation in a child's room. This furniture always needs reviving, and older children will enjoy the experience of creating a mural for their own furniture. In addition, you can profit from a child's uninhibited approach to design.

To expand the idea of murals even further, imagine a wall mural that includes furniture as part of the overall design. Exotic painting techniques, whether they portray a single flower or a multi-colored mural, need not limit the function of the furniture. Superhard transparent finishes will seal creative work, making it as practical as it is attractive.

If the prospect of applying your special talents and techniques to mass-produced, utilitarian furniture makes you shudder, design and create your own furniture. As furniture becomes art, and art, furniture, the artist/craftsman is able to ignore our conventional labels and become totally involved in the creation of his or her very personal environment.

A contemporary approach to decoupage was used on this furniture cube. Magazine prints and photos were cut, sealed, and glued to the cube to form a collage. Many coats of decoupage finish protect the cube from wear.

CREATIVE SEATING*

Macramé, stitchery, appliqué, patchwork, weaving, batik, rya, silk-screen printing, plus all other forms of creative textiles offer imaginative alternatives to usual seating materials. Your only limitation will be to retain the strength and comfort provided by the original seating material.

Macramé. This ancient art of knotting provides strength along with excellent creative possibilities. Macramé seating can replace almost any type of traditional seating material from caning to needlepoint. Several types of chairs are particularly adaptable to macramé. Chairs with perforated frames that once held woven cane are best suited to macramé if the holes are large enough to accept a strong cord. After you have determined the feasibility of your knotting material, begin by counting the number of holes in the front chair frame. Divide this number by two to determine the number of *single* cords needed to macramé the entire seat. Next, determine the correct length of each single cord by measuring the distance of the frame opening from front to back. Multiply this number six to eight times, according to the size of the cord and the number of knots planned. This sum indicates the length of every single cord but the first. The first cord will need to be twice as long, since it usually doubles as a knotting cord and a knot-bearing cord throughout the entire design.

The diagram below indicates one method of threading the cord through the holes in the front frame. The first cord is threaded from the bottom of the left-hand corner hole. Its shorter end (equal to the other doubled cords) will be threaded up through the next hole on the right; see first step in diagram. The holes to the right show how to thread to achieve the pattern shown in the chair seat illustrated on this page.

The diagram to the right indicates the technique for threading macramé cord into a perforated chair frame. The finished seat is illustrated below.

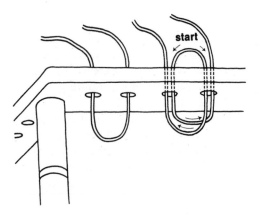

---

* **Note:** If you are not familiar with basic techniques for creating textiles suggested in this section, refer to other books in this series: *Step-by-Step Macramé, Weaving, Crochet, Knitting, Printmaking, Rugmaking*, etc.

This beautiful chair was given a second life after the original seat had worn out. Constructed simply of horizontal double half-hitches, the finished macramé seat was placed in the chair frame with the reverse side up. As with pressed cane, a shaped reed spline holds the new seat in place.

The examples here illustrate three different approaches to creative seating. A mass-produced footstool was the base for the patchwork hassock by Rose Dwight. Joan Tallan's two-color silk-screen design enlivens an ordinary director's chair. The appliqué slip seat by Rose Dwight demonstrates a way to express your individuality with older furniture.

The finished example has been knotted with horizontal double half-hitches to provide maximum strength with a minimum of stretching. After each row of knotting, the knot-bearing cord passes down through the adjacent hole in the side frame, then up through the next hole to begin another row.

When using macramé for furniture reseating, tie each knot as tightly as possible—there will always be some stretching after the seat is in use.

Prewoven, pressed cane can also be replaced with macramé. You will need to follow the instructions for the insertion of regular prewoven cane, the only difference being that macramé seating is pressed into the spline opening. Read and understand the instructions for pressed cane seating (page 24) before you begin. Remember, the knotting cord must be thin enough to fit into the spline opening, but strong enough to hold the weight of a person. Now, make a pattern of the seat opening, overlapping the spline by 1 inch in all directions. Pin this pattern to your knotting board and fill the space with your own creation. Open macramé patterns are not advisable for this type of chair. Test the strength of your knotted material as you progress.

Chairs that have exposed seat rails or worn fiber-cord seats and are rather dreary reproductions of traditional furniture are perfect candidates for macramé. Approximate the length of each single cord as in the previous perforated chair frame. Cut, then tie each doubled cord to the front rail using the reversed double half-hitch. Also use the reversed double half-hitch to secure each succeeding row of knotting to the side rails. Finally, use this same knot to fasten the seat to the back rail. Thread the loose cord ends from the top to the underneath side of the seat. Knot these cords, making a row across the bottom seat rail. After one or more rows of tight knotting, it will be safe to cut and glue the cord ends under the previous knotting.

Slip seats. Chairs with open frames are commonly found in junk stores. They may have been constructed with an embossed leather seat, but over the years substitute seating has left nail holes and many scars. When there is no slip seat, begin by cutting a ⅜-inch-thick piece of plywood approximately 1 inch larger than the seat opening. Then cut an identical shape from ⅛-inch hardboard. Place the plywood over the seating frame and measure inward 1 inch from each corner and mark. Clamp the plywood and hardboard pieces together and drill through both as marked. Separate, and set aside the hardboard piece.

Insert bolts through the plywood and countersink them level with the surface. Glue the bolts in place with epoxy cement. Pad the plywood seat. You are now ready to consider your textile design.

Woven, macramé, or crochet tapestry designs relate well to this type of chair. In addition, patchwork, batik, appliqué, or silk-screened fabrics give you a full range of techniques from which to choose.

To finish the slip seat, cover the padded plywood with your newly created fabric and tack or sew it in place. Position the completed slip seat over the chair opening and attach the hardwood base, securing it with lock washers and nuts.

Canvas chairs. The canvas indoor-outdoor chair also offers limitless possibilities for creative techniques. The plain canvas covers of a director's chair can be totally replaced with a heavy handwoven fabric or a rya or macramé material. Draw a pattern first, using the original canvas covers as your guide. Don't forget the back section must be stitched to slip over the posts, and dowels may need to be reinserted into the sides of the seating material.

An easier but no less creative approach is to make a loosely woven, crocheted, patchwork, or knitted fabric that will partially or totally cover the original canvas. Strength need not be a consideration here, but beware of bulky fabrics that will spoil the comfort of the seat.

In addition, canvas coverings lend themselves to the direct application of printed or dyed designs. To tie-dye, start with a colored or white canvas cover. Fold and tie, then dip into a dyebath as the dye instructions suggest. Cool dyes, which do not need to be heated, will not shrink prefit canvas and are available at most craft and hobby stores. Batik dyeing works in a similar way, except that the color areas you wish to preserve will be covered with wax. Melt a mixture of paraffin and processed beeswax in a double boiler until it is flowing warm. Use a brush or tjanting tool (for drawing with hot wax) to draw your design. Dry the wax, dip into the dyebath, and rinse as directed. Allow the canvas to dry. Repeat this process for each additional color. Place canvas cover between papers and press with hot iron to remove wax after design is complete. Or use both tie-dyeing and batik to produce an interesting fabric. In fact, consider combining several textile techniques to create an outstanding fabric for your furniture.

Bibliography

Berger, Robert, *All About Antiquing and Restoring Furniture.* Hawthorn Books, Inc., New York, New York, 1971.

Brazer, Esther S., *Early American Decoration.* 2nd ed. Tudor Publishing Co., New York, New York, 1962.

Constantine, Albert Jr., *Know Your Woods.* Charles Scribner's Sons, New York, New York, 1972.

Edlin, Herbert L., *What Wood Is That?: A Manual of Wood Identification.* The Viking Press, New York, New York, 1969.

Fales, Dean A., Jr., *American Painted Furniture, 1660–1880.* E. P. Dutton and Co., Inc., New York, New York, 1972.

Higgins, Alfred, *Common Sense Guide to Refinishing Antiques.* Funk and Wagnalls, Inc., New York, New York, 1969.

Kinney, Ralph P., *The Complete Book of Furniture Repair and Refinishing.* Charles Scribner's Sons, New York, New York, 1971.

Nimocks, Patricia E., *Decoupage.* Charles Scribner's Sons, New York, New York, 1968.

Also see the following books in the Golden Press *Step-by-Step Craft Series* for techniques relating to Creative Seating:

Cosentino, Geraldine, *Bargello,* 1974.

Phillips, Mary Walker, *Macramé,* 1970.

Schachner, Erwin, *Printmaking,* 1970.

Wildman, Emily, *Crochet,* 1972.

Znamierowski, Nell, *Rugmaking,* 1972. *Weaving,* 1967.

A combination of batik and tie-dyeing was used to transform a white canvas cover into an original fabric design for a butterfly chair.

Photo Credits

We wish to express our appreciation to the following for their help in providing photographs for this book:

 2: Photo courtesy of The American Crafts Council's Museum of Contemporary Crafts, New York, New York. "The Love Affair or The Cow Pasture Bed" by Michelle Gamm Clifton appeared in the "Sewn, Stitched and Stuffed" exhibition 4/12—6/10, 1973.

 6: Chairs and tables by Cohasset Colonials, Cohasset, Massachusetts. Reproductions of Shaker originals; photo taken in the Fruitlands Museum, Harvard, Massachusetts.

65: Courtesy of the C.H. Tripp Finishing Company, La Jolla, Ca.

68: Courtesy of Connoisseur Studio, Inc., Louisville, Kentucky.

70, top left: ©1973 Downe Publishing, Inc. Reprinted by Permission of *American Home.*

72: Collections of Greenfield Village and the Henry Ford Museum, Dearborn, Michigan.

75: Courtesy of *Family Circle* Magazine; photo by Mort Mace.

The following photos are by Nancy Howell-Koehler: 18, right; 25; 26; 36; and 60, bottom. The photo on page 64 is by Bill Patterson.

All other photographs by John Garetti.

Suppliers

Most of the tools and materials mentioned in this book are readily available at local paint and hardware stores. Special items may be ordered from the following suppliers. Unless otherwise noted, all sell both retail and mail order.

General Woodworking Supplies

Albert Constantine and Son, Inc.
2050 Eastchester Rd.
Bronx, N.Y. 10461

Craftsman Wood Service Co.
2729 S. Mary St.
Chicago, Ill. 60608

Unfinished Furniture

Cohasset Colonials
Cohasset, Mass. 02025

Furniture-in-the-Raw
8 Rewe St.
Brooklyn, N.Y. 11211

Storehouse
3106 Early St., N.W.
Atlanta, Ga. 30305

Unfinished Wood Furniture Store, Inc.
4728 Wilmington Pike
Dayton, Ohio 45440

Seating Supplies

Cane and Basket Supply Co.
1283 S. Cochran Ave.
Los Angeles, Calif. 90019

Craft Service
337–341 University Ave.
Rochester, N.Y. 14607

Newell Workshop
19 Blaine Ave.
Hinsdale, Ill. 60521

Peerless Rattan and Reed
  Manufacturing Co.
97 Washington St.
New York, N.Y. 10006
(mail order only)

The H. H. Perkins Co.
10 S. Bradley Rd.
Woodbridge, Conn. 06525

Upholstery Supply Co., Inc.
P.O. Box 6756
5242 Shawland Rd.
Jacksonville, Fla. 32205
(mail order only)

Veterans Caning Shop
550 W. 35th St.
New York, N.Y. 10001

Yellow Springs Strings, Inc.
P.O. Box 107
Yellow Springs, Ohio 45387